DEGREE IN NINJA

A College Student's Guide to Study Strike and Succeed

DEGREE IN NINJA

A College Student's Guide to Study Strike and Succeed

By Ryan Penneau

www.TakeBackCollege.com

The nation's leading organization in college success presentations

Degree in Ninja – A College Student's Guide to Study, Strike and Succeed

Printed In North America

This Edition
Black and White Paperback, Spiral Bound, Workbook and Book Combination

ISBN - 978-0-615-52171-8

Other Editions
E-book
First Edition Bound Paperback
Second Edition Bound Paperback

More information available at www.TakeBackCollege.com
Direct Email to Speaking@TakeBackCollege.com

Dedication

I do what I do for students. My commitment is to the students of this world and the potential before them.

I have the fortunate opportunity to travel the country and talk to thousands of students every year, and I do it because from Florida to California, New York to Texas and the whole of the heartland, I get to hear students and their stories, their hopes, their ambitions, their barriers and their opportunities. It is in building relationships with these students that I get to experience the puzzle that is our nation's future.

To the student reading this book, you're part of the puzzle. We need your piece to complete the picture. Understand you have the world at your fingertips. That's what the college experience is all about. Make it your experience!

This one is for the students. I'm pulling for you.

An Introduction

A young man had a best friend in his dog. He loved it dearly and the two were the best of companions. One day, the dog fell ill and the boy went to see the town's vet. The vet looked at the dog's condition and told the boy to administer two tablespoons of medicine every evening and the dog will become well again.

From that point forward, the boy would wrestle the dog between his knees, pry his mouth open with one hand and pour the medicine in his mouth with the other. As soon as he would be done, the dog would spring away upon being released. "Sorry, pal," the boy would say.

One night, while wrestling to get the dog to take his medicine, the dog knocked the bottle and it spilled everywhere. Amidst the boy's frustration, he saw the dog return and begin to lick up the medicine.

Two major things that I've come to learn throughout my life are:

1) **There is nothing more powerful than when one person requests from another, 'Teach me what you know', and**
2) **Human beings are creatures of growth, and we naturally desire to gain through learning. People love to learn, but we don't always enjoy the format in which that learning takes place.**

TABLE OF CONTENTS

A NOTE FROM RYAN

In my years of working in the world of student development, leadership education, experiential education and job preparedness, I have had the privilege of exploring the factors of student success. I have interviewed students, listened to their feedback, paid attention to the trends, built relationships with professors, staff and faculty, read the journals, and even went back to school just to truly understand student motivators, success principles, and the ins and outs of a fulfilling college experience.

When I was in college, I didn't participate in clubs, activities, special events or much else. I thought 'leadership' trainings, workshops, and speakers were kind of an irrelevant rah-rah. I bulked up on credits, changed my major six times, didn't develop many substantial relationships with professors or peers, graduated, and earned my first job with a nonprofit that focused on all of the things I avoided while in college; student development and leadership.

I began as a speaker and mentor for students, and I came to learn rather quickly that student development is my life's passion. It's exciting! It's fascinating! It's different! It's difficult! And it's a whirlwind of unbelievable potential and possibility.

The more I worked with students, the more I found that there are a lot more students out there that were just like me when I was in college. And as I met these students, I just wanted to say, ***COME ON! CHECK OUT HOW FREAKING COOL THIS COLLEGE THING CAN BE!!!*** And a mission to put education back into the hands of students has since driven me to do everything within my power to give students the tools, tips and strategies to THRIVE.

I was the last person you'd ever see reading a college success book, and still probably wouldn't. So in writing a college success book, I wrote one selfishly. I wrote one I would want to read. The cool thing is that I believe my design and approach in this book will move you to think and possibly even a new outcome of what your college experience can be.

Enjoy!

To your success, your fulfillment and the following of your passion. Cheers!

It's good to know you better.

Ryan Penneau

A Post-Introduction, Introduction. And some general things you should know before we get to the fun.

What's with the ninja thing?

It was inspired at a campus I was visiting. A student of mine said 'you ninja'd that test' and I thought, "Everyone wants to be a ninja at some level or another: ninja artist, a ninja teacher, a ninja psychologist, a ninja business owner." People love the ninja, and the more I thought about it, the more parallels came to my awareness. Ninjas are masters at what they do; students should be experts in their field of study. Ninjas are committed, disciplined, focused and dedicated to bettering themselves. Not one part of me thinks that any of those are bad things. Ninjas are cool. You're cool. Cool plus cool equals double cool.

We pause for a reality check moment.

I know, right? A pause on the first page? This book is fast like lightning, which makes sense because ninjas are fast like lightning. Since this book is about what it takes to be a College Success Ninja, I think it's only appropriate to make it fast as lightning. In the spirit of uncanny fastness, I think it is in our best interest to pause and collect ourselves before the awesomeness of this book and all the incredible information knocks us into a coma-seizure. Coma-seizure? Yes, coma-seizure.

Which reminds me! I have to give a fair warning! Implementing all the stuff in this book all at one time will certainly kick you sideways. If you try taking this on all at once, your brain will overload like a freight train. It's best to take it in a little at a time.

If this was me, and I know because I am, I would approach this book in bite-sizes. I would implement anything because I would trust the author knows what he/she is talking about. I would, however, implement little by little. Don't over-commit, under-deliver and ultimately stress yourself out because you didn't do what you said you were going to do. Prioritize the first things you want to tackle and do them. If you do everything in here, I virtually guarantee success, a fulfilling college career and a meaningful job afterwards. The bottom line is that the turtle won the race, the rabbit didn't.

Speaking of Ninjas...Yay women!
Please understand that when I wanted to share my success strategies for college students, I wanted to model the book and mentality around a figure that was cool, savvy, fast, effective and ultimately, kind of bad-ass. The figure that came to mind was a ninja. When I say ninja, I'm definitely not excluding ninjettes. I think ninjettes are crazy-freaking-cool. Ninja is an all-encompassing word for those that practice the art of nin and those that practice the art of ninette.

Um...what else? Oh! Let's be upfront.
The stuff in here takes work, it takes discipline, and it takes an effective approach to your post-secondary education. Some of the tips in here are crazy-weird! And you'll probably think, "What's the point?" EASY, young grasshopper! Don't jump the gun. You'll understand the answer at the end of the journey. Not all lights were meant to be seen at once.

Test this stuff out and see where it takes you before you discount the advice. Although you're all capable of it, not all of you are going to become ninjas. That's just the way it works. There are two kinds of people: Ninjas and Not Ninjas. Individuals with the true spirit of the warrior will make it through the storm of a thousand tornados; others will fall to the wayside as they sway to the way of the winds. You're successful because you do what no one else will do or you're not because you do what everyone else does...which is usually nothing more than average.

Different
Success is not difficult, it's different. The tips, suggestions, strategies in the book, they're not difficult, they are different. It's not difficult to get a healthy amount of sleep; it's different from everyone else for you to get done what you need to get done and not get distracted, so that you get the sleep that will give you the right amount of energy, clear mind and health. For the next

few years, do what no one else will do so after college you can do what no one else can do. Success is not ordinary, but it's not difficult- it's just different.

Metaphors and Analogies

A true ninja guide wouldn't be anything without them. So, like a bear to the honey of the bee, enjoy some of the visuals I piece together. The advice part of this book ...that's all GOLD. The metaphors part...purely entertainment and a little bit of distraction.

Lastly, My Mission, My Message, My Meaning, My….point of self-promotion

I think students deserve a level of success that is reflective of what they truly desire to accomplish. I think a more fulfilled student creates a better quality of life for themselves. From that, I believe that same student will demonstrate their gratitude for life by contributing to the betterment of his or her community. I believe students have far more potential within them and before them than they are aware of, but so many facets of the college experience are left unchecked, unexplored and neglected. I work with thousands of students every year, and my mission is to ensure they have the tools, capacity, and competency to create opportunity and put the responsibility of living a passionate, fulfilling life on themselves (on yourself). It's going to take a revolution.

REVOLUTIONS DON'T WAIT. And neither will your life. I'm in the game to TAKE BACK COLLEGE! And I am calling out to the students nation-wide to join me on this (nonviolent) demonstration to bring college back to its purpose of preparing people for the life of their dreams; and it's not going to take overthrowing the Dean. *It's going to take initiative, action and purposeful intent to deepen your college experience.* This will require you to go beyond the classroom to develop what you need to develop for where you want to go and what you want to be. It's 100% on you, no one else.

That's why we need to create a ninja army. Ninjas are unstoppable. Ninjas are awesome. Ninjas have the nin and ninette essence that is unbeatable. So let's go to battle! But, a mother pterodactyl doesn't throw its baby out of the nest without feeding the baby first, right? You need to know the mission, you need the proper training and tools for success, and you need to be ready for whatever comes your way.

Your Ninja Training Begins Now!
May the peace of a thousand cherry blossoms, swiftness of an ocean current and strength of a tectonic plate be at your side and within your heart!

"If you don't believe that ninjas have REAL ULTIMATE POWER, than you better get a life, or, I tell you, something's going to be up in your grill. Get wise, man. All I'm saying, get wise. It's an easy choice if you ask me."

-Jimmy, a 13 year old

The Haters! There are constant daggers being thrown at up-and-coming student ninjas. These daggers are filled with evil poison that will make your mind foggy, sad and ineffective. You may even puke in your mouth if you get hit with one of these. The more young ninjas that fall to these daggers, the more our battle is lost.

In all seriousness, the 'go to college' environment is not one of fun in this day and age. Bad PR is among many of the factors crushing student spirits. Let's have a look at what some people are saying:

Economist (Let's just call him John), so John refers to colleges as "failure factories," where dropping out is the norm.

"We could be doing a lot better with college completion just by working on our colleges," as (Let's just call him John too) John, Whitehouse education advisor,

Headline from USA Today: "Is College Worth It?"

Same headline, different article, ABC News: "Is College Worth It?"

More headlines: "COLLEGE: The BIGGEST GAMBLE of your LIFE!"

Even more headlines "Don't Take on The Debt!"

From an online Blog - College is a bunch of rooms where you sit for two thousand hours or so and try to memorize things. The two thousand hours are spread out over four years. The rest of your time is spent sleeping, drinking, and trying to get dates.

Even faculty are on this bandwagon, "I've come to the conclusion that a college/graduate school education may be America's most overrated product." – *Anonymous* Career Counselor

In 2005, young people (ages 18-25) in the US gambled $67 billion-- economic analysis shows that college is a financial mistake for more than half of the American young people today.

"If you see a college recruiter, put your head in the sand and hold as still as possible so they can't see you; they are coming to punch you in the face." Ryan Penneau...but I jest, I jest :)

As if the some of the mass media didn't already do a great deal to scare everyone into giving the nation education-phobia, the haters are hiring top secret laboratories to CAPTURE young-ninjas and study them like rats. NOW, GET ON YOUR RUNNING WHEEL AND DRINK FROM YOUR GIANT SIZE DRIP WATER BOTTLE!

40% of students report they would not attend their college again if given the choice
-ABC News

The United States does a good job enrolling teenagers in college, but only half of students who enroll end up with a bachelor's degree (54% of students graduate)
National Center for Education Statistics

75% of college students lack skills to perform real-life tasks.
CNN

64% of all workers under the age 25 are unhappy with their jobs. TNS Global Market Research

70% of high school students fail to graduate "college ready"
Manhattan Institute for Policy Research

TUITION IS GOING UP. That's pretty straight forward.

50% of all college students report feeling so depressed at some points in the last semester that they had trouble functioning. Suicide remains the second leading cause of death of college students.
The American Psychiatric Association

$27, 803 is the student average cumulative debt for a 4-year undergraduate degree. (students are basically starting out broke before they even get started!)
2008 National Post Secondary Student Aid Study.

Which is kind of cool if you think of how much we're investing and not having for debt; which is further cool that we can toss around that kind of dough! I think this means we take education pretty seriously. Not serious enough? Some would say, some would definitely say.

89% of student illness, weight gain and weaker immune systems are STRESS related. *Education-Portal.com*

"45% of students show no improvement of critical thinking after two years of college. After 4 years, 35% showed no improvement in critical thinking."
Collegiate Learning Assessment

"1.4 million people with college degree out of work, compared to 1.2 million high school drop outs. More high school drop outs have jobs than college graduates."
CNN.com

THIS STUFF REQUIRES A BIT OF A CRITICAL EYE!!!!

Critical Thinking

Alright, young ninja, get your grappling hook, we are going to climb this one.

"1.4 million people with college degree out of work, compared to 1.2 million high school drop outs. More high school drop outs have jobs than college graduates."

Duh! Ninja! Focus Up!

If you dropped out of high school, what is your personal belief in the kind of job and career responsibility you should have?

Alright, so now, let's say you have a college degree, would your standard for a job be a little higher than that of a high-school drop out?

Do you see what would happen if people just opened up their minds and let anything get dumped in? We'd all live in a state of constant insecurity and….AGH-ness. Fear and insecurity are not the ways of a ninja. Ninja's live in confidence, purpose, and understanding that challenges will come, but with a little critical thinking and action, any obstacle can be subdued.

Let's chop off the head of another one:
40% of students report they would not attend their college again if given the choice.
So, is this saying that students wouldn't have attended THEIR specific college or wouldn't attend college in general? What goes into this? Are they saying once was enough; they don't need to get another degree? Are they regretful because the wrong influences went into why they enrolled in their specific college? Or did those students just NOT LIVE COLLEGE RIGHT?

NINJA! Many students regret college because they don't do it right! They go in, go through the motions, and don't master anything. They commit the time to aimlessly wander. **This book is designed to give you strategies to be effective so that passive experience takes a backseat to your will-do, initiative-oriented action plan to getting the most out of college.**

A Short Story - The Healthy Young Man

Someone approached the young man and told him, "You don't look so good, I think you may be sick."

"I don't feel sick," responded the young man.

"Are you sure, because you don't look well, my friend; but if you feel well, perhaps you are," and the passerby continued on their way.

The boy thought about how he may have looked to the passerby, "Is my skin pale? Am I sweating or tired? Could I be sick, I certainly don't feel sick." He continued on his way as these thoughts ran through his head and he began to feel stressed and felt his stomach turn, his heart began to race, and he felt hot. "I AM SICK! I feel it. I hope it's nothing serious. I cannot be out of commission for even a day because I'd fall too far behind; but I must be sick."

The man sought out the passerby from before and went to him, "I am sick. I don't know how you knew, but can you help me?"

"Of course, of course," the man replied. "Here is a medicinal cure that I came up with. This will help you with your ills."

The man took the medicine and began to feel better instantly. "Amazing! I feel better already!"

"You look better," the man said.

The next day the young man woke up feeling great! And on his way into town, again he passed the same man that cured him. The man saw him and said, "My, I had thought you'd be cured beyond today. You don't look so good, you should come by again for more medicine."

The man thought to himself that he may again be sick. Since yesterday he was sick without feeling sick, today could be the same. So he went to the man for more medicine.

This cycle continued for days to the point where the man could not wake up without first taking his pills before he felt good about the day.

Really?!

If we listened to all of the garbage that is tossing college around like it is of no value or a waste of time, would you really be here? Of course not!

On the other side of the spectrum, however, would you ever date someone that had so many red-flags as it seems like college does? Probably not.

I know you've heard some of these negative things, and some of these negative things have brought college attendance and application rates down. And if you don't take the time to really THINK, this negative picture the world paints of college might bring you down to. So I ask...

Why are you in college? Why are you here?

I ask this question to my classes when I teach and I am always amazed by the answers I receive. Everything from 'I don't know' to 'Because it's just the thing you're supposed to do' and 'I am passionate about becoming x' or 'my parents told me to'.

But what about you? Let's get the thinking starting. Why are you here?

Why Is Critical Thinking So Important?

It is easy to enter a new environment and situation with a ring through our nose, just waiting for someone to tie a rope through it and pull us along to wherever they want us to go. It's like that old saying, "If you don't have plans of your own, you'll become part of another person's plans." Guess what 'another person' has planned for you. Not much.

When I first entered the personal success world, I was in love with a research study that I heard several speakers reference over and over and over.

The story went like this. Harvard conducted a study of one of their graduating classes where they asked 10 percent of the class to write down specific life goals for their career, income, family, and overall happiness, and the other 90% did not. A follow up study took place with the class 25 years later that found that the 10% of graduates that wrote their goals down collectively earned more than the 90% of graduates that did not.

CAN YOU BELIEVE THAT? Writing goals is so powerful that the 10% of graduates that actually did, earned more than the 90% that did not!

THAT'S A POWERFUL STAT!

I kept hearing this powerful story over and over again, and I said to myself, I can't wait to share this story at my next talk about being a rock star goal setting ninja. I began to prepare my presentation and I NEEDED to include that story, but I forgot some of the details. Since academic journals and research are always published, however, I figured this should be an easy internet search.

Not only was it an easy search, but I quickly came to find that the whole thing was fiction! For 50 years, speakers have been referencing each other as the source to the story and none of the thousands of speakers that ever shared that story ever did their own thinking on it.

That's not altogether bad. Thousands of people have been inspired and taken on goal setting as a means to their goals because of hearing that story, and goal setting is good! In fact, I'm a proponent of it. But I do think it's interesting how easily led we are.

You need to be able to think for yourself. Allow ideas to flow in like an ancient breeze through the branches of a cherry tree, but don't let that breeze knock you out of the ground. Be open to ideas, think about them, see where the fit, test them out, ask questions, see where the journey of looking deeper will lead you. Usually the road to discovery is one that you will find tremendously beneficial.

College is not just a time, it's your time.

If there is one thing I've learned in life it is that if you feel a cliché coming on, you need to release it otherwise it just wells up inside you.

College is not just a moment, it's the moment. These are 'the best times of your life'. I used to hear that ALL THE TIME, and every time I heard it, I just rolled my eyes. In college, I couldn't stand some of my roommates, I didn't like that I didn't develop a strong social network, I was disappointed in myself for not getting involved, and too much time slipped through my fingers to mindless activities instead of invested towards exciting opportunities. I could have exited college with a huge database and network, as a truly passionate and experienced individual in my field of work, and with a stronger bond and relationship with staff and faculty. But (drumroll please) I didn't.

College years are the best times of your life. You can test, poke, and prod any of the things you've ever said that you should do. You can start a business, an organization, an annual fundraiser. You can develop research, write books, form amazing relationships with brilliant people. You can form the memories worth mentioning and the wins worth repeating. **College isn't just a moment, it's the moment for you to do amazing things.**

Thank you for allowing me the time to get that little pep-talk off of my chest. 90% of the conversations I have are about students and student success; these are the things that drive me. I wouldn't be able to write the next 200 pages or so without a quick 'Yay, you can do it, this is awesome, you're awesome, we're awesome, yay for awesome' kind of speech.

We cool?

Cool.

Thanks for letting me indulge.

A Nin-like Essence….

I spent an evening watching some national news broadcast. You know, one of those late-night primetime things where most of the introduction graphics are blue and grey, there are a lot of serious expressions, and a journalist gets to the *HEART* of an *ISSUE*!

On this particular broadcast, the ISSUE was GRADUATES Ain't Got No Jobs...but it was much more professional and scary sounding, and now for the *HEART* of the *ISSUE*, introducing Sally Stevens (I don't know her real name, so I made up the name Sally). Sally was not a ninja.

Sally was interviewed because she doesn't have a job, she spent over $80,000 on a college education, and she is over $100,000 in debt. Oh, one other thing, she had to move out of her $800/month studio-apartment to move back in with her parents because her no job-ie-ness couldn't afford rent.

Every time Sally was on camera, her energy was in the toilet. She was slumped over, mumbled, complained, and blamed. She talked about her four years of school being a waste and that she **regretted it**. The journalist was sympathetic, "Geez, did you ever think you wouldn't get a job?"

"No."

"Wow, that's awful. And now you're in debt, moving in with your parents, what are you going to do?"

Let me take it from here Mr. Journalist, Sir. Sally will probably do what she did when she was in college: NOTHING!

Suddenly the TV caught on fire. Probably because I was using my ninja mind powers to light it up.

Why don't you ask sally if she was involved in some student organizations? Why don't you ask her if she took it upon herself to get noticed by professors by speaking up and participating in class? Ask her if she sat in the front row or hid in the back behind a laptop! Ask her if she attended opportunities to network with professionals! Ask her if she trained for the real world by going beyond the classroom or if she just went to class doing the bare-bones minimum to skate through to a degree.

SHE'S ON NATIONAL TV and instead of wearing professional clothes and positioning herself as being energetic and outgoing to the MILLIONS of viewers (potentially hiring viewers), she's wearing some baggy long-sleeved T-shirt, hunched over and completely unenthusiastic about ANYTHING!

"So what do you think of your college years?"

"They were a waste."

"Would you go back?"

"Never."

"Do you think this is in any way your responsibility?" *No one asked her this question.*

"Gee, I'd love someone like that on my team to help my company grow, go, gain and kick butt." Said no employer ever!

THE ESSENCE

The essence of nin is a skill just like anything is a skill. It takes effort and practice and trial and expanding your comfort zone to get there. You feel a ninja's energy, their aura, their glow, their spark. They bring life; they don't take it. That flare brings a confidence, something dynamic that makes the average person think to themselves, "What is it that they have that I don't?" They know how to ninja, and that art of ninja was practiced, consciously developed and consequently is getting them noticed (if they want to be since ninjas only get noticed when they want to). This book is the beginning of a journey to developing that nin.

- Start to…create positive meaning and value from what you read and the seemingly mundane.

- Start to…be hungry for more education and the betterment of yourself.

- Start to…be willing to sacrifice who you are for who you are capable of becoming.

- Start to…endure challenge and discomfort. Growth is not without effort.

Pressure Points

What is a Pressure Point?

A pressure point is an area on/in a person that generates significant pain or weakness when struck in a specific manner. Effects of a ninja striking a pressure point include black out, forget who you are, acne, loss of breath, fatigue, death, rabies, pterodactyls swooping in, picking you up and feeding you to their babies, failing out of college, nuclear fallout, the national debt, pain, concussion, heightened blood pressure, a pack of wild chimpanzees hunting you through the forest, or possibly even worse. So get wise, and take the initiative to protect and prepare these aspects of your world before they are fatal weaknesses that will slow you down or knock you out.

I would TOTALLY keep these protected at all times; otherwise, CHOP TO THE FACE! and you're done, my friend. You're cooked like bacon.

College has Pressure Points Too.

If unprotected, weakened or attacked, these pressure points will cause severe consequences. It's best that you stay conscious of them, protect them, and actively strengthen your defenses against them.

Pressure Point
Mental stress and fatigue plague the average college student and they are caused by more than just poor sleeping habits. Emotional stress from new relationships, management of old relationships, over-commitment, lessened demands for physical activity, newfound personal responsibility and the consistent message of 'college – it will make or break you' all impact the health and clarity of your priorities and your thoughts.

Pressure Point
Social Chaos. If you thought high school relationships were complicated, you have no idea what's ahead. And get this, young ninja, I'm not just talking about romantic relationships, I'm talking all relationships. Your parents aren't with you every day. Professors are more casual than teachers. What's the balance between professional mentor, colleague and instructor? Dorm etiquette? Peer pressure? Identifying healthy or not healthy relationships. All of this stuff comes with this new frontier of developing who and how you define yourself for the next four years. You are who you surround yourself with.

Pressure Point
Lifestyle. Ninja, I wouldn't even consider 90% of your lifestyle an actual lifestyle. Habits are hard to develop when every Tuesday and Wednesday, class starts at 8 am, every Friday, class starts at 12:00 and ends at 4, Monday nights are spent up until 2:00am writing reflection papers, meals fluctuate from 1 a day to 2 a day to 5 a day and as often as the winds change. There's not enough time, and certainly not enough money, and you're wearing the same underwear for the third week in a row because every time you want to do laundry, the machines are full. Lifestyle? Ninja, it doesn't have to be like this.

Pressure Point
Uncertainty is that thing the river said to the lake. It said, "I need some time to find myself," as it pours into the ocean. The ocean! Get it!? I don't know if you did, but I laughed. See, because the river is pouring into something that's even bigger, vaster, and more unknown. C'mon! Give me at least a smirk because that was

clever. As you pour into this 'ocean' you are mixing, blending, meeting, and experiencing all things new, different, and sometimes weird. New found independence, personal responsibility and independent decision making can create feelings of self-doubt, second guessing and sometimes an inability to see a light at the end of the tunnel. Stay with me, by the end of this book, we'll be chewing on this cement brick of a stressor with our ninja teeth.

Pressure Point
Personal foundations carry with them aspects of a college career that are mentioned during things like orientation, leadership workshops, and speakers, but aren't often given enough time and serious reflection by students. By the time most students realize how important this piece truly is, they are almost drowning in the need to catch up, get back on track and start over. It's easier to build what you need to build now than to wait until life has you in a place where you need to fight your way back from in a rut to an even playing field, let alone to get ahead of the curve. To summarize, it's easier to stay in shape than to get back into shape.

Pressure Point
Career expectations. You know that thing, that reason as to why most of us enroll in college in the first place, so that we can become success ninjas and make a killing in any economy! Get your head straight, Leroy.

Yes, college is the time to develop yourself and gain in experience, but bottom line is that college is a vehicle to advance your lifestyle, personal fulfillment, and skills through a career path. Will I be able to afford these loans with my career choice? Is this what I really want to do the rest of my life? Is my field hiring? What do I need to do to get the job? How can I ensure a career now and not have to wait until the last four months of my senior year? Am I doing the right thing? Do I want to do this? If these questions haven't raced through your head like a tiger chasing a monkey through a fire, then you are one of a gamillion (that's an actual figure). This is big. More to come!!!!!!

Pressure Point

Academic outlook is bleak. Remember high school? Math, science, read a little, write a little, sprinkle in some foreign language and leave your trust with the high school because there are state standards that need to be met. Those were the good days. College can be a labyrinth of what and who and where the heck am I going, doing, becoming?

"He got a cord at graduation! Look at me, I have no cord! I am cordless. I will never get a job. I will never get married because I don't have a job. I will never have kids. People will hate me because I can't relate to my peer group in 15 years. All because I have no cord, no GPA, not the right amount of credit, the wrong credits.

So, yes, academics can create stress.

What you must remember is that you can master these elements like the metal smith masters gold.

A sensible speech from the ancient masters of long ago.

To know that you are ignorant is best;
To know what you do not, is a disease;
But if you recognize the malady
Of mind for what it is, then that is health.

The Wise Person has indeed a healthy mind;
They see an aberration as it is
And for that reason never will be ill.

Lao Tzu

Ninja Symbols

Ninja One Touch Knock Out Power Move
Power Moves are quick tips hits that don't require practice and that you can implement almost immediately.

Ninja Shadow Master Secret
A ninja's effectiveness is in their ability to stay hidden and use subtle, fast, super-secret methods and techniques to achieve their mission. These techniques will take conscious effort to develop over time.

A Ninja Explains
Allow Ninja to be your guide and mentor through your ninja degree training. Each topic discussed in this book has its own moments of confusion, chaos and crap in relation to college. Ninja will explain how each subject of discussion relates to you.

Ninja in Training Challenge
You're not a ninja yet. Don't get ahead of yourself. Master these challenges, master yourself.

Reflections from a Dojo Master
Straight from a master. The author of this book traveled many secret journeys, climbed high and low, swam many oceans and flew through many trees to find guidance and reflection from these masters of ninja success.

How this Book Works

This book doesn't work. It's a book. Books don't do anything on their own. The only way any tip, strategy or idea works is if you take action. Consistent and ongoing action...so, like, more than once.

Get Uncomfortable

This is a GUT CHECK. Some of the activities in this book will be way out of your comfort zone, but it is in stepping outside of your comfort zone that the most success occurs.

If you want to be stronger, you don't get stronger by lifting weights that are comfortable for you. You get stronger by lifting weights that are uncomfortable, weights that push you, weights that sometimes cause a little bit of pain when you pick them up. Pick up the heavy and uncomfortable weights offered in this book. You will like the results regardless of the discomfort.

Be Ready when Opportunity knocks

College isn't meant for you to be comfortable and complacent, it's meant to challenge and grow you so that you can expand your opportunities. This book was designed with the same intention. I'm not interested in getting you in the right place at the right time. I'm interested in ensuring that when you are in the right place at the right time, you are the *right person* to take advantage of that opportunity. The only way to ensure you're that right person is to grow yourself by expanding your comfort zone. Embrace the ideas in this book, test them out, and see what you are capable of.

First Skill Set

Personal Foundations

As surprising as it may seem, the average student actually has more time and less commitments while attending college than when they are in their first career-oriented job.

YOU HAVE MORE AVAILABLE TIME NOW THAN YOU WILL AFTER COLLEGE! It's easier to find 20 minutes for pleasure reading now than it is after college. It's easier to develop the habit of going for a morning run now than it is after college. It's easier to carry a standard for work ethic and time management into the real world than it is to start from scratch the minute you are out of college and tossed into a new world.

The next several years is about setting some real standards for who you are, what you represent, and the legacy you plan to live and leave. The practices and commitments that you develop are imperative to your future success. You must take the active approach to ensuring these building blocks are unshakable, unbreakable, and immovable. Put some real thought towards the habits you want to develop and some serious reflection towards your life goals, plans and steps you need to take to get there.

Each of the initiatives that are discussed in the Personal Foundations section take a lot of focus and energy in order to transform them from good intentions to habits.

Know the individual within yourself that you want to represent, the accomplishments you want under your belt, and the way in which you want to be remembered; don't wait, start building now.

Ninja Preparing

"Before everything else, getting ready is the secret of success."
Ninja Henry Ford

Ninja Philosophy
- **An ill prepared ninja is not prepared**
- **If a ninja doesn't get ready; ready gets it**
- **A prepared ninja creates the right circumstance; a ninja that doesn't prepare is created by the circumstances that come**

Ninjas are born ready. They know that challenges are going to come and attack like a jackrabbit in the morning sun. They understand that preparing is half the battle. Ninjas understand that if they aren't ready, some other ninja will be and will ultimately reap the most rewards.

Preparation isn't a onetime thing and it doesn't happen in one day. And if you don't prepare, things will suck.

Ninja Shadow Master Secret
Visualization techniques have proven to increase effectiveness, productivity and preparedness, manage behavior, reduce stress, and increase personal ability in areas of test taking, health, public speaking, and more.

Enemy of the Ninja
Keep a watchful eye on time. It's a skulky S.O.B. It is easy for a ninja in training to say, "I do not have fifteen minutes to study. I do not have ten minutes to visualize. I do not have thirty minutes to exercise. I don't have time for another class or a meeting with a professor." If you don't have the time to be effective and do what you need to do to get prepared, you certainly won't have the time to catch up from being behind due to being ineffective. NUNCHUCK your excuse of 'no time'!

Ninja Explains Preparedness

Preparing for college is work, and a true ninja doesn't just hand off the job. Preparing yourself for the lifestyle and responsibility of college needs to start now; and this practice and preparation is a necessary key to your success in college. Passing a test requires prior preparation. An effective use of tomorrow's time means preparing for tomorrow today. Effective meetings and discussion requires knowing the notes and research beforehand. Getting the job at an interview means preparing for an interview by researching the company, researching current trends, and understanding best practices for potential responsibilities. Hell, that's what college is really all about; years of preparing you for the career and lifestyle of your dreams. The more you know before any opportunity, the more you'll gain from the opportunity when it comes.

Ninja One Touch Knock Out Power Move
College is the breeding ground for the habits that will stay with you throughout the rest of your life. What you sow today you will reap tomorrow. Every day of college, fit this in to your schedule: 20 min exercise, 20 min reading of not required materials, wake up early, study 20 min, always be on time. Imagine what you could develop for yourself.

Ninja in Training Challenge

You have much work ahead of you. Every day of your college career will host at least one class discussion, org meeting, or community debate. Your challenge is to prepare for 15-30 minutes through reading the materials, doing internet research on the topics, and studying your notes. When the opportunities present themselves for you to share, you'll significantly benefit from knowing the materials/topic and adding to discussion. Sure, you could 'wing it'; but that will catch up to you.

REFLECTIONS FROM A DOJO MASTER

Hello, young grasshopper. You come seeking wisdom and guidance, it shall be rewarded.

It's not your professor's responsibility to prepare you for the real world, for a job, or for a career; they are responsible to you, not for you. It is your responsibility to go beyond the classroom and learn more, find more, experience more, ask questions and engage in the learning and the preparing experience!

It's easy to enter college thinking, "If I just go to class and do well with grades, I'll be set for the dream job, easy money, big title business card."

That's simply not true. Your professors are responsible for equipping you with the ideas, insights, personal experiences, and curricular foundations necessary to developing framework and reference point in your industry; they are not responsible for your success, the actions you take, or the character you develop.

You must go beyond the classroom to develop a platform for your success.

When you combine curriculum with the exercises in here…WOAH, young warrior. WATCH OUT! You will be a much desired, and highly paid ninja.

To your success, grasshopper.

Ninja Planning

"People with goals succeed because they know where they are going.
It's as simple as that."

Ninja Earl Nightingale

Ninja Philosophy
- If you don't plan, you will go by someone else's plans
- Plans allow ninja to strike when ninja wants to strike
- A ninja that fails to plan, plans to fail

Do you know why you never can find a ninja? You never find a ninja because ninjas are so disciplined at planning that they always know where you will be looking. They are always two steps in front of you and ready to drop your no-planning butt in a ninja-second. The early bird gets the worm; the ninja sets his sights on the bird, eliminates the worm, pretends to be the worm, and when the bird comes by, HEEEYA, ninja eats bird. Bird didn't plan for that! Ninja did.

A lack of a plan creates a lack of purpose. Less than 10% of ninjas practice goal setting. That's why less than 10% of people are true ninjas.

Ninja Shadow Master Secret
Look at your plan like a building; not like a line across a page. When you look at a line, you see events that are disconnected from each other. When you look at your plan like a building, it'll be clearer what you need to do now in order to build upward.

Enemy of the Ninja
No plan means that you are vulnerable to whims, time wasters, and shiny objects. A ninja shouldn't have time to chase shiny objects. If you do not have a plan, it will be very easy to be frivolous and distracted with your time and not accomplish anything. With a plan, you are committed to not just working, but working on the right things. Ninjas aren't born, they are made through clear, defined, achievable goals.

 **Ninja Explains PLANNING**

Every aspect of your life should have a plan; a money plan, health plan, education plan, career development plan, success plan, relationship plan, family plan, future plan, hobby plan, travel plan, reading plan. Not a lot of people take the time to make plans, which is why it is hard to get up in the morning. Planning cultivates and illustrates purpose and goals which are a lot stronger than just another day at class. When every day has a purpose and is a step towards accomplishing your goal, every day is manageable. Even when you get distracted or off track, it's easy to know what to do to get back to your goals, just stick to the plan.

Ninja One Touch Knock Out Power Move
Get real, half of the people reading this book won't know how to do laundry on their own let alone know their life purpose. Don't get stressed about not knowing your life plan, career plan, family plan, a figure it out plan, the point is, make a plan. Don't beat yourself up if you don't know exactly what you want to work towards.

 Ninja in Training Challenge
Pick three areas of your life and make a plan for them with SMART goals. SMART: Specific, Measurable, Attainable, Realistic, Timely.
Specific – What EXACTLY do you want to accomplish?
Measurable – If you can't measure it, it's not worth doing.
Attainable – Intention is great, but get real, you won't end poverty over night; what can you do now with what you have?
Realistic – Not easy, but do-able.
Timely – If you aren't gaining momentum and accomplishing something within a timely manner, you'll get tired chasing. Time limits create a sense of urgency and stronger commitment.

Reflections from a Dojo Master

Hope is not a plan. It's not an option. It's not a possibility. It's not going to get you far.

You can't hope yourself through a test you didn't study for. You can't hope yourself into a major that fits you if you didn't talk to professionals in the field and find out all that you could about it. You can't hope your way into a great letter of recommendation from a professor without showing up for class. And you certainly can't hope your way into a job without a fairly extensive demonstration of how you can be a relevant piece to their puzzle.

Too often we numb ourselves to hope. Hope Hope Hope.

Hope is great when that's all that's left, but rarely, and I do mean rarely, are we ever left with absolutely nothing: no feet for walking, arms for doing, brains for thinking, words for writing, mouths for saying, or initiatives for taking.

The old man was having his evening pipe. While his son was cleaning after dinner, he smelled something burning. Turning to his dad, he said, "Dad, you're beard is on fire! Do Something!"

The old man said, "I am! Can't you see I'm hoping it rains."

Hope is a great attitude, but you have the wherewithal. Make a plan. Do something about it.

To your success, grasshopper.

Ninja Time Management

"This *time*, like all times, is a very good one, if we but know what to do with it."
Ninja Ralph Waldo Emerson

Ninja Philosophy

- o **Time passes, not even the ninja can stop it; but the ninja knows where he/she stands at the end of it**
- o **A ninja with a list is too busy to focus on being awesome, but even then, ninjas are still awesome**

You're busy. So are ants. Of the two, which accomplishes more? Ah, good question. Do you know where your time goes? Have you ever spent a week documenting where all your time went? Ninjas know where their time goes. Everyone is given the same amount of time. A true ninja is in control of how that time is used. An impatient or undisciplined ninja puts their time to waste.

Crappy ninjas let time master priorities; true ninjas allow the priorities to master time.

> ### Ninja Shadow Master Secret
> There are thousands of tips and tricks for time management, do one Google search and you'll find them. All time management, however, can be boiled down into three simple steps: recording, managing, consolidating.

Enemy of the Ninja

Some ninjas do not know where their time goes. Since they don't know where it goes, they don't know how much they start with, and more and more of it will begin to escape from them. Sleep in for 20 more minutes, watch 15 minutes of tv in the morning (most of which is channel surfing and commercials in the morning), spend seven minutes picking out clothes, and 18 minutes dinking around on Facebook. You spent the first hour of your day with nothing accomplished. I know a ninja that is better with a bo-staff and is making more money than you because of this.

Ninja Explains TIME MANAGEMENT

You know what they say, "I'll start this when things slow down." Karate chop yourself in the face every time you think that! Here's your first lesson of time management: life doesn't slow down. It keeps moving, you must keep moving too.

Everyone is given 24 hours in a day, no more, no less; how you use that amount of time is up to you. You will hear 'I don't have time' from every friend and colleague you meet in college. EVERY ONE OF THEM! Be the ninja that always has time for the important stuff because you are a master of your domain, you know how to effectively kill projects, papers and studying, and you don't waste time on anything, you invest it in measurable, accomplishable goals.

Ninja One Touch Knock Out Power Move
Remember what ninja says! Managing time isn't like managing money; you only have a finite amount of time regardless of how you manage it. Solution? Manage yourself! Don't waste time on things that pull you from focus, distract you, or aren't directly related to accomplishing a goal.

Ninja in Training Challenge
Study, eat, exercise, wake up, go to bed at the same time every day! When your responsibilities are routine, time management is easy.

What's the priority? Facebook updates or research papers? You have time! It's all about the value you place on goals.

Lastly, DOCUMENT YOUR TIME! Journal where every hour, minute, second goes.

I blog. And I received RAVE reviews from this post. So I said, why not share it with more people!

Have you ever watched a zombie movie? I love zombie movies! LOVE EM! And every October, I host the all weekend, every weekend, zombie movie marathons!

All zombie movies follow a very particular formula. They all start with, of course, a zombie
apocalypse. This epidemic spreads from one person to another through infection and disease. Then the zombies start to take over. That's when we meet a group of people. The group of survivors enters the scene. And as always, one of the people in the group is accidentally bitten in some heart wrenching moment of suspense. The group eventually finds out that said member is infected, at which point the members of the party split into two groups: those that see the infected individual as a threat… get rid of 'em, and those that see the person as a person…keep 'em. Usually they hold on to the individual who is actually a threat, he/she bites some of the others and threatens the survival of the group and only one or two survive.

What's this to you? So we all have zombies in our life...but check this out...what do you do? Kill 'em or hold on to 'em? Most people hold on to their zombies because, like in the movies, we are too emotionally attached to let go. We have these time killers in our lives that are just wasting away and infecting our productivity and opportunities to thrive. It's time you identify your zombies because if you don't, your zombies have the potential of turning you into an automated, mindless zombie.

At first, Facebook was really a cool thing to do that people would spend a bit of time on to respond to a few messages and move on with their days. For most, however, Facebook has become an automatic, brainless activity that consumes, on average, an hour and a half of a person's day every day. This is a useless zombie.

In business, we continue to spend two hours a day responding to emails. We don't pick up the books and study because wc think four hours rehashing the day or catching up on celebrity buzz is 'just a typical part of the day'. We don't prioritize on the most effective important priorities of the day, but we catch up with friends at the grill. The people that survive the movies eliminate the zombies. The people that don't survive, are too caught up in emotion and say "well this is how we've always done it."

I believe that anyone can find two hours in their day to use on more effective or bigger priorities. Document where your time is going on a weekly basis; then, if there are things in your life that aren't contributing to your ability to thrive and survive, to stand up and stand out, then it's time to get rid of those zombies!

Time to go zombie hunting before they take over your livelihood. Right now, those zombies are costing you progress and success!

Quick Tip
Invest into two computer monitors!

Did you know that having two computer monitors can increase your work productivity and effectiveness by 30%-40%! It's true! In having more than one monitor, you can easily access documents, files, and papers with one, while doing research on the other without the hassle of minimizing or hiding what you're working on. Setting up two monitors is easy to do too! Find someone in your res hall that is skilled with computers or just go to your university's tech center! Seriously! Do this!!! It's the easiest thing you'll ever do to increase your productivity.

A Ninja's Master

"Mentor: Someone whose hindsight can become your foresight."
Anonymous Ninja

Ninja Philosophy

- A ninja could teach class if he/she wanted to; for the time being, however, it's better to let the Doctor speak their piece
- A ninja knows they can do it on their own; but knows a ninja professor brings more credibility to opportunity

Remember, you are a ninja-in-training with access to some of the most intelligent and networked ninja professors in the world; don't waste this opportunity. You may not like some of the stuff they teach you; but you don't use the blade without the knowledge of how. Your ninja professors aren't going to hand you the grade because you show up; it will take your ninja focus, ninja skills, and ninja discussion points to receive the title of true ninja.

Professors are mentors and doors to the future; but careful, there is a fine line between friends/colleagues and buddies/pals. Learn as much as you can from the ones that have gone down the route you intend to go, but don't abuse the relationship.

Ninja Shadow Master Secret

At the end of four years you'll want letters of recommendation and references. Where do they come from? Professors. Decide what the ideal letter of recommendation looks like for you; now follow that letter and do what it takes to make it true! Build strong relationships with professors early on.

Enemy of the Ninja

Thinking the professor doesn't notice. Professors are masters. They are ninjas too! Their power of observation and attention to detail is powerful and often underestimated. They pick up on everything: how you hold yourself, where you sit, how you act in class, if you're late, your participation and beyond. To think a professor doesn't notice, is like believing pandas are coming off the endangered species list. Be aware of how you project yourself in class.

 Ninja Explains **PROFESSORS**

Your professors are your doors to the future. That's right! Professors are a lot more than the people that teach the classes. These individuals are connected to the community, to businesses, to networks, associations, boards, and other colleges; and are ultimately your greatest resource in applying for jobs and continued education. Get to know them, meet them, ask questions in class, participate in conversations, visit them during their office hours; they are your references, mentors, and ultimately the 'hand that feeds you'. Always be sure to mention your career goals, objectives and dreams because they'll be your support and lifeline to them!

Ninja One Touch Knock Out Power Move
Don't ask for extensions. Don't make excuses. Ninjas are honest. As much as you might be a master at mystery; professors can see through bull and cut to the core with their blades of experience. They aren't your parents; they don't care that your dog died and that's why you failed the test.

Ninja in Training Challenge
Professors aren't your buddies and they're certainly not your parents; but they can be phenomenal relationships. They don't have to learn to get along with you, you have to learn to get along with them. Having a close, mentor-student relationship with professors isn't bad. In fact, it's something you should strive for since they'll be your asset.

REFLECTIONS FROM A DOJO MASTER

Yes, sitting in the front row improves GPA. Although there has been no study demonstrating that sitting in the front row causes grades to increase; there have been studies showing the sitting in the front row allows certain things to happen, **WHICH CAUSE YOUR GRADES TO INCREASE!** Why?

Sitting in the front causes you to:
- be more attentive to the lecture,
- less distracted by others,
- more focused on the content and delivery versus watching what 100 students in front of you are doing,
- you can hear and see much more with much less effort than if you were sitting in the back,
- you are in the professor's field of view
- you're more likely to engage and participate in open dialogue and questions,

which all ultimately cause your grades to increase and make a stronger impression on your professors. *SIT IN THE FRONT!*

It demonstrates an eagerness and WILLINGNESS to be in class which will carry over into other aspects of your life!

Ps. Do EVERYTHING YOU CAN TO NEVER EVER EVER ASK FOR AN EXTENSION! Seriously, <u>Make reasons as to why you followed through, not why you didn't</u>.

To your success, grasshopper.

Ninja's Responsibility

In life, if you knew you were making history, you'd pay a lot closer attention.
Anonymous Ninja

Ninja Philosophy
- o **Ninja's are where they are because they want to be what they are**
- o **A ninja at fault is a ninja with power**

No one can kill a ninja, they cannot die. Therefore, the greatest battle you will have, ninja, is the battle you have within yourself. That little ninja voice inside you that looks outward and says, "Of course you can't; look at what you're up against." The true ninja doesn't listen to that voice but instead listens to what they know is true, that every opportunity is there for the ninja to take.

Ninja, you succeed or you fail; both times it's you.

> ## Ninja Shadow Master Secret
> Don't play it safe. Most people don't take risks because they don't want to take responsibility if there are consequences. Jump on in, ninja. If you hit your mark, you hit your mark. If you hit a Jeep, you hit a Jeep. Either way, be ready to own up to it.

Enemy of the Ninja
Our ninja soccer team won! Hurray! *We* won!

Next game, they lose. Geez. *They* lost.

You take the good with the bad young warrior. You want the gold for the success, but can't handle the pain of the fall? Life's not about either or. You get both the rewards and the consequences for your choices and actions. Don't blame, complain, point the fingers and play victim. Be the person that can stand up in all situations and own up for the things you do or do not do. A great sense of pride and confidence comes along with the ability to own up to life!

 **Ninja Explains RESPONSIBILITY**

Everyone knows what they *should* do. That intuitive feeling that tells you that you should study, you should go for a run, you should put down the video games, you should say you're sorry, you should edit that paper one last time; and whether or not these things do or do not happen is entirely up to you. No one else. College is your responsibility. You don't get to take responsibility for just the good parts either. Where you put the effort is your choice. Take complete and 100% responsibility for the choices that bring you where you are.

Ninja One Touch Knock Out Power Move
Learn from failure, learn from success. Neither of them define you. Neither of them determine your results as you move forward in life. All that will define you will be what you learned from the successes and the failures. Don't beat yourself up for the stumbles and don't celebrate yourself too much for the victories.

 Ninja in Training Challenge
If you had the chance to do it all over again, would you? Would you do anything differently?

When you think back to your younger training days, Ninja; you'll begin to realize the moments in your life where you could have made a different choice. If you want something different years from now, don't focus on what others should do for you; focus on what you can do now. You don't know just what the implications will be.

If I said, ten years from now, you will be the same person you are now, how happy would you be with that? It's time to own where you are, where you want to be, and what YOU need to do differently.

Ninja's Integrity

Be yourself no matter what they say.
Ninja Sting

Ninja Philosophy

- Ninjas do what they say they will do
- Ninja's actions reflect who they are
- Ninjas are happy to be themselves, and are themselves
- Ain't no carbon copy

In all that a ninja says and does, let one thing be true: the ninja is true to him/herself. We spend a lot of time talking about preparing yourself professionally and personally for the next steps. About what college is 'supposed to be like' and about the new challenges you will face and have to adapt to; but one thing must be remembered though it all, college is a time for you to be authentically you! As much as this is a time to explore what's 'out there' take some time to find what's 'in there' as in 'who you are'.

Ninja Shadow Master Secret

Be yourself. Easier said than done….You might want me to elaborate on this. Honestly, if you went from this point forward with one thing consistent…who you are…you will be successful.

Enemy of the Ninja

Politics are involved in everything that two or more people are involved in, and they can be nasty. Politics can be good; but they can also be destructive… And as our world grows in competition with one another for that promotion, job, raise, girlfriend, boyfriend, professor's nomination and beyond, politics can easily take shape and begin a behind the scenes battle of manipulation, drama, and dishonesty. In that, it will be hard not to fall into the 'dog eat dog' world; but ninja, stay strong. The short term gain of selling out your integrity is not worth the long term impression people will have of you. When in doubt, be true to yourself, and allow your actions to reflect the positive side of you.

 **Ninja Explains INTEGRITY**

Integrity is the personal characteristic that guarantees all other characteristics. Personal success is often the result of who you are and whether or not all aspects of your life are in cooperation (not at odds) with one another. Your integrity, the person you think you are, say you are and act on is truly what matters in life. Do do not falter when in difficult circumstances. Follow through without excuses. Do what you say you will do. Your life reflects the heart which reflects the mind. Be true. This doesn't mean always right, this doesn't mean always good; this means that you are who you say you are. Ninja, you must take responsibility for shaping and crafting your integrity. It's your shadow. It's your reflection. It's what people will come to depend on.

> ### Ninja One Touch **Knock Out** Power Move
> Integrity is consistent to your values. Have you developed your values? Identify your five major core values; the qualities or characteristics that speak to who you are and the legacy you will leave. That's the easy part. Step two; ensure all areas of your life reflect those values.

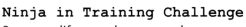

Ninja in Training Challenge
See your life as a house; each room representing a different piece of your life (personal, professional, family, etcetera). Now, ask yourself the question, "can you knock down the walls of that house and still be the same person as you were when the walls were up?"

Transparency is the key to integrity. Ensure all of your lives run parallel with each other. It will cause a great deal less stress for you.

Ninja's Never Surrender

Play the game for more than you can afford to lose... only then will you learn the game.
Ninja Sir Winston Churchill

Ninja Philosophy

- o **There *were* dinosaurs; there *are* ninjas...if dinosaurs were ninjas, we'd still be watching the skies for pterodactyl attacks**
- o **A ninja may lose an arm, another arm, kidney, eyeball, foot, ear, shoulder and tongue; but the ninja never walks away**

The water rolls, flows and moves down river. Over rapids, around boulders, off bends, over corners, through dams water always makes its way to the sea. Ninjas flow like river, pour like rain, erode the cliff like acid snake venom and always get to where they must go. Ninja you are water, isn't that powerful and calming all at the same time? Most agreed.

46% of students do not graduate college. Apparently that boulder in the river looks too big. Find a way around it, through it, over it. Let no boulder stop you.

Ninja Shadow Master Secret

Set up a reward system for yourself. It helps to motivate and feed your drive to accomplish. It is also a way to allow yourself some psychological wins on your road to success versus feeling accomplished when the big picture is completed.

Enemy of the Ninja

Ninja, you can defeat an entire army with nothing more than a paperclip and a rubber band. Ninja, you made it this far! All of the past tough times, you've survived! You are a one out of 6 billion chance; and we're not going to blow smoke up your butt, but you can make the impossible possible. Who can? You can. Your financial dreams, professional success, family life, educational excellence are available to the few that are daring enough to do the impossible. Do the impossible. You were born to thrive not just survive.

 Ninja Explains **NEVER SURRENDER**

Exactly. Failure is not an option. Finish what you started!

Any ninja master worth their weight in gold will throw you to the wolves without a lifeline, and that's what college is all about. There are no easy outs, no trap doors, and no disappearing tricks. You go in head-first with the decision made to succeed. Ninjas don't surrender. Ninjas don't quit. Ninjas do whatever it takes to find that last bit of adrenaline to cross the finish line. It might be hell to get there; but the rewards don't come just before you finish, they come after you finish. Again, if you have the wherewithal to understand this text, you have the duty and responsibility to not give up on your dreams, goals or self.

Ninja One Touch Knock Out Power Move
Stay ahead, not behind. The temptation to give up most often comes when we feel behind. The homework piles up, the grades aren't what we want, the paper isn't done, and no one likes feeling hopeless so it's easier to say 'this just isn't for me'. Stay on top if not ahead of the game. That's why you get a syllabus.

 Ninja in Training Challenge
When a ninja has defined their ultimate purpose; they will do what it takes to get there. Often times we lose hope and are willing to give up on our ninja dreams because life gets too tough, and we lose sight of our goal. Develop a compelling and unique purpose; once you know what it is, look at every day and every challenge as another step towards your goal. Your life will transform from a series of challenges to a road of purpose and prosperity.

Quick Tip

Want to learn the quickest way to low self-esteem? Not following through or finishing what you started.

Regardless of what you think, if you don't finish what you start or do what you say you will do, it will add unnecessary stress to your life. If you think you don't have time to finish something, think of it this way, **you don't have time to stress and be less productive if you don't finish what you set out to accomplish.** This is the smallest of the small, to the biggest of the big! **Finish what you start, and stop thinking, 'wouldn't it be nice to have this done', and just get it done!**

Where do most great ideas go?

I believe that most great ideas go to the grave because they are never acted on, and they stay great ideas and great intentions. Intentions and results are two different things. No one is going to talk about 'what you were going to do' at your funeral. Stop talking about what you want to have done and what you want to finish. GET STUFF DONE!

Ninja's Development

If you wish to achieve worthwhile things in your personal and career life, you must become a worthwhile person in your own self-development.

Ninja Brian Tracy

Ninja Philosophy

- It's not about what happens to the ninja; it's what the ninja does about it
- Ninja, grow like tree. Rest like bear. Eat like tiger. Learn like elephant.

Ninja, work to lift a 70lbs dumbbell. You would argue that it is not a goal of yours. I could argue, 'Sure, but imagine the person it will make you become'. This is the nature of development. Personal development is a process and sometimes it takes doing odd things to grow in competencies that you may not be the expert in. Growth is not about obtaining something, it's about the person you become along the journey. At any moment be willing to sacrifice who you are for what you are capable of.

Ninja Shadow Master Secret

Remember your whole life ninja. You are not just a part, but you are a sum of parts. A sum of many skilled ninja parts that work together to make you a ninja. Do not neglect parts of your sum. Your financial, physical, emotional, relational, intellectual, personal, professional, spiritual are all aspects of you that you should actively develop. Do not neglect.

Enemy of the Ninja

It's easy to think that everything a ninja needs to know he'll learn in class; after all, you are studying a specific field for a specific degree so it should be safe to assume you classes will cover everything. Ninja, investment in this idea is equivalent to the belief a puppet has no master. You must learn beyond class.

By the time you graduate, most of what you learned your freshman and sophomore year will no longer be relevant. That's two years you need to make up for through immersing yourself in your development. Develop yourself.

Ninja Explains DEVELOPMENT

A standard level of growth, education and development will get you standard results. Making the most out of your life, however, is uncommon among people; so it's going to take some uncommon effort and uncommon action to earn an uncommon lifestyle. What is your continual personal development plan? Does it extend beyond college? It should. Even when you have a job the rest of the world is going to keep on moving, learning and staying relevant. The easiest way to exceed, excel and remain invaluable in your career field is to stay on top of it, to be the expert and to continuously develop your confidence, attitude and skill. I guess if you wanted to sum this up in one sentence: ALWAYS GROW!

Ninja One Touch Knock Out Power Move
Summer doesn't require ninjas to continue education; the ninjas that stand out on their resumes are often the ninjas that take that summer and turn it into an educational opportunity. Ninja, don't allow the heat of the summer allow you to wither and die within your development. Do something with it so you are MORE of a person because of it.

Ninja in Training Challenge
Ninjas are some of the most cunning, clever and knowledgeable warriors in existence; and they aren't born that way. They develop their depth of knowledge systematically, continuously, and always.

A ninja studies everything that could pertain to his field of interest.

Be on top of the knowledge in your field; continuously develop, grow and learn so that you can be a master ninja dragon awesome.

Reflections from a Dojo Master

According to the book, 'The Global Achievement Gap', American students are far behind their international counterparts in the development and utilization of soft skills. In a recent study of 10,000 college grads measuring their ability to function in the areas of the 'soft skills', only 12% were measured as excellent and a whopping 32% were deficient.

College is a very formative time for you. Your brain is still growing and developing and there are major aspects of who you are that will come to full realization if you give the appropriate efforts towards them.

How do you measure on your ability to be independent, self-motivated, solution-oriented? How are you at communication, critical thinking and teamwork? Do you understand emotional management, empathy and leadership?

If these words mean nothing to you personally or if you feel like some of them are completely lacking as a skill, you need to know that 1) YOU CAN develop and get better in these areas, and 2) college offers several opportunities for you to do so.

To your success, grasshopper.

Study, Strike, Succeed

Ninja, get this done with the speed of a bear.

Why do I want to graduate college?

_____

_____

_____

_____

_____

What must I achieve from my college experience?

_____

_____

What are the three most important and crucial things that I want to achieve because I attended and completed college?

_____

_____

_____

What are the three most important things that I must do in order to obtain the above?

_____

_____

_____

What are two actions I can commit 15-45 minutes to every day for the next year?
1) _____
2) _____

At the end of the year, I will have what because of the above actions (365 pages written, 30 books read, a small business started, et cetera).

_____

_____

_____

What are the most valuable qualities and characteristics that you represent and that you would to everything within your power to never falter from?

Characteristic   What does it mean to you?   How do you
                                                     Demonstrate it
                                                     When confronted with difficulty?

Now, remember this:
I understand that I will not always align with these values, because even the circus ninja that spins 15 plates can be thrown off balance from time to time. If I fall off balance, I will be quick to remedy the occasion, forgive myself and seek to do better in the future of my ninja duties.

A "why" is the pulling force that puts your focus on a big picture goal. The people you will impact, the lifestyle you deserve, the relationships you'll have, the accomplishments you create, the legacy you leave, the difference you make. Everyone has a why that pulls them through the most difficult times. What's your why?
_____

_____

_____

_____

_____

_____

Do some reverse engineering. It's simple, easy, and smart. Reverse engineering puts you on target towards a goal. It states, "This is where I want to be after x amount of time; here are the steps I need to take to get there."

I've been challenging students, interns and employees to do this for years because for many, it changes the paradigm and approach to their habits, activities and goals.

The Ideal Letter of Recommendation
For the next few years, young ninja, you have the opportunity to network like a something or other.

To whom it may concern,

I am writing in regards to_____, and his/her application for
_____. I have known him for _____ years, in a
_____ capacity. I am more than pleased to
recommend him/her for this position, and feel that he/she is beyond qualified in
the following areas.

He/she has participated in the following campus events and organizations:
_____ , _____ , _____ , _____ . In each of these
activities, he/she has displayed many characteristics to be commended, including
_____ , _____ , _____ , and _____ . In class, he/she has always made
a strong impression with his _____ , _____ , and _____ . I
have continually enjoyed working with him in and out of class time due to his/her
respectfulness and eagerness to learn. I can clearly see his/her strong desire to be
the very best he/she can be in his/her field. I can attest to his/her strong

personality and ability to be a natural born leader after witnessing his/her participation in   .

Most importantly, I can confidently say that he/she will fit perfectly with your company/program/opportunity after witnessing him/her complete/direct/display . It is with the utmost pleasure and pride that I confidently recommend him/her for   .

Sincerely,

Dr. Mentor

(Note, this is a great start to a template, but you should take it upon yourself to write your own. What do you want focused on? How you interact with people? Work ethic? Your solution-mindedness? Your deep knowledge of a topic or industry? Whatever it is, write it and make it happen!)

Where is your time going? Track every activity of yours for the next four days. Some of you will only have to do this for one day to find out what's going on in your world.

5 am		9:30		1:30		6	
5:15		9:45		1:45		6:15	
5:30		10		2		6:30	
5:45		10:15		2:15		6:45	
6		10:30		2:30		7	
6:15		10:45		2:45		7:15	
6:30		10:30		3		7:30	
6:45		10:45		3:15		7:45	
7		11		3:30		8	
7:15		11:15		3:45		8:15	
7:30		11:30		4		8:30	
7:45		11:45		4:15		8:45	
8		12		4:30		9	
8:15		12:15		4:45		9:15	
8:30		12:30		5		9:30	
8:45		12:45		5:15		9:45	
9		1		5:30		10	
9:15		1:15		5:45			

List your current 'zombie' activities?

_____

_____

_____

Total the amount of time towards each 'zombie' activity.

_____

What can you do to begin taking 'zombie' time and putting it towards the priorities and goals in your life? Where will that put you in 30 days? Where will that put you in two years?

_____

_____

_____

Personal Notes from This Section

_____
_____
_____
_____
_____

Questions I still Have

_____
_____
_____
_____

How I intend to get answers

_____
_____
_____
_____

Things I want to discuss with a professor, mentor, or advisor.

_____
_____
_____

To improve in my ninja skills and to better my abilities of becoming an ultimate success ninja, I will take it upon myself to follow through on the following discipline/commitment/action each day this week:

_____

_____

_____

_____

I understand that it may not be easy, it may be a little different, but if I'm to truly master the art of nin, then let the above statement be burned in steal by the dragon of a thousand daggers. I will complete by the end of the week.

Second Skill Set

Managing Stress

Better grab an umbrella, because I'm about to rain down some facts.

Stress is the leading cause of illness among college students, causing 98% of illnesses diagnosed by doctors and nurses of young adults. Around 23% of college students are diagnosed with depression, with feelings of stress and feeling overwhelmed as the leading causes. Students face terrifying amounts of debt, work deadlines, the potentially slim chance of obtaining a job, and a significant drop in the formation of healthy relationships (healthy relationships being essential for emotional wellbeing, mental and physical health, and coping abilities).   Therefore, it's not a surprise that 70% of 300,000 students from 200 different colleges surveyed by the Higher Education Research Institute report feeling that their stress levels are significantly higher than their peers.

There are three types of students in the world of stress: First, those that get it and FREAK OUT! Second, those that get it and manage it really well through exercise, time management, and better health practices. Third, those that get it and internalize it, look like they are under control and completely are not.

Did you catch the common theme among the three groups? Every student feels and will feel stress. And like I say about floods, if you knew one was coming, you'd do everything you could to prepare. Well, stress is coming, and it's better to prepare for the flood than to try to manage the flood while wanting to keep your head above water. Let's get this stress stuff put together, in line, and out of play.

Ninja's Stress

"Sometimes a headache is all in your head. Relax."
Ninja Hartman Jule

Ninja Philosophy
- **The venom of the stress snake kills ninjas over time, not at once**
- **Ninjas train and prepare for stress like a village prepares for a flood**
- **A stressed ninja will eventually flip-out, not in a good way**

With so many demands on a young ninja: discipline, training, spying, studying, classes, exams, weaponry, technique, calls home to ninja parents, managing money, ninja friends, and GPA (Grab Punch Accuracy), it's easy for a ninja to flip out. The stressors of your ninja training are parasites to your effectiveness. Just one starts feeding from you, no big deal; but over time, as more and more start to attach and suck away, ninja starts to lose some blood, sense of self and their smile. Kick stresses butt.

Remember, ninjas never strike as effectively when clouded and stressed; but can take out a whole army if stress is channeled properly.

> ### Ninja Shadow Master Secret
> You must know what triggers stress in you. It's different in every ninja. Don't let stress build up, otherwise it will eat your soul and take your enjoyment out of life. Find a hobby and maintain it!

Enemy of the Ninja
Inaction in a young ninja will internalize stress versus doing something and getting rid of the stress. Take action and stress will take flight.

Ninja Explains STRESS

Stress comes in a lot of forms and it's common within college students...and most adult ninjas for that matter. Stress, however, isn't always a bad thing. Episodic stress that is triggered during moments where stress is necessary - before a test, before a basketball game, getting ready for an important interview – these are all moments where a little jolt of adrenaline is good! Stress can become a bad thing, however, when it evolves from episodic to a continuous state. Unmonitored stress quickly transforms into a person's way of life where getting out of bed can seem like a chore. If you don't take the time to identify and combat stress early, overtime it will lead to burn out, lack of motivation, and an overall sense of hopelessness. Ninja, stress need not be something that defines who you are.

Ninja One Touch Knock Out Power Move
Let's get real. Chances are you won't cut the caffeine, you won't get 7 hours of sleep a night, and you won't walk around saying positive affirmations to yourself, all of which reduce stress. But you can keep your living space clean, maintain healthy friendships, stay in touch with family, and decrease alcohol intake, all of which are proven to reduce stress.

Ninja in Training Challenge
Take stress seriously. Many ninjas look at overwhelming amounts of stress as the normal routine and feeling of life; it's not. You can enjoy life even though it feels like the weight of the world is on your shoulders. Develop a stress management plan. Like a gazelle. A gazelle's plan is eat and make babies and run like hell if a fire breaks out. Be the gazelle. Plan and prioritize for tomorrow, and be ready to do something with the stress.

Ninja Health

"We can no longer be useful when we are not well."
Ninja Samuel Johnson

Ninja Philosophy

- A ninja is one with their health
- A healthy ninja has more options when attacking, dodging, evading, eluding, spying, chopping, and otherwise than a sick ninja

Contrary to most beliefs, only a handful of ninjas can chisel their muscles from their own flesh and heal from it; the rest of us have to discipline, eat right and sleep. A ninja's body is his or her greatest weapon and tool. The ninja that can soar like the nighthawk will catch it's prey. The ninja that stalks its prey like the overfed domestic cat that has lost its edge, reflexes and speed will be eaten by a wolf. That's the circle of life.

It's not about the years, it's about the mileage. Keep your body sharp, and your mind, emotions, and attitude will follow.

Ninja Shadow Master Secret
Not only is physical activity good for you; but it also conditions you to love giving effort! College will take effort, sometimes going beyond what you think you can do. By knowing your psychology behind pushing your limits, you'll be ready for more.

Enemy of the Ninja

Ninja! LOOK OUT! You're surrounded by killer samurai warriors, the sworn enemy of the healthy ninja! Ice cream socials, campus cafeteria food, late night snacking, inconsistent sleeping patters, increased alcohol consumption, less physical activity, quick meal, less vegetables and fruits, increased sugars and caffeine are all ready to pounce on you! It seems like a lot to battle at once, but this battle is nothing compared to the battle of going from poor health and overweight to good health and in shape.

Ninja Explains **Proper Health**

Take care of your body and your body will take care of you. Approach college because you want to work hard, and invest yourself towards THRIVING. That's the right college attitude. The wrong college attitude is, "Whatever." If you go in to college just to get by and don't worry about your health, then you'll have other things to worry about. With the new environment, changes, no home cooked meals or required gym classes; it's easy to forget about your body's strengthening. 18-25 is the time you set the tone of your health. Get in the right habits on your health so that the stress of college doesn't bring on illness.

> **Ninja One Touch Knock Out Power Move**
> Drink more water! Don't ever be thirsty. Why? It controls weight-loss and maintenance, it keeps your heart healthy, it significantly increases your energy and lessens fatigue, it maintains healthy skin, it helps flush out toxins, allows you to maintain your focus on goals for longer periods of time. Always bring a water bottle to class.

Ninja in Training Challenge

Develop a normal exercise routine. Endorphins are natural chemicals in the body that are produced when a person is exercising. These babies are your open door to stress-relief, protecting the body from pain, and preventing everything from depression and fatigue to the common cold *(that's right, when endorphins are pumping, you CANNOT catch the common cold).* The best way to trigger endorphins is through exercise; this is the best for the long-term because it builds up your insulin production and immune system.

Ninja's Balance

Ninja Jim Rohn

Ninja Philosophy

- **A ninja will always have many things happening, give the appropriate time and effort to the priorities**
- **A ninja thar doesn't balance, will lose the battle and maybe the war**

Only advanced super ninjas can be in seven places at once. You must understand the art of balance. A typical college ninja has A LOT going on and A LOT more depending on them, how you manage this all will determine much of your success.

Where ever you are, that's where you'll be. You can't control what's going on somewhere else. Be everything to the moment you're in.

> ### Ninja Shadow Master Secret
> A ninja is very much demanded from in all areas of its life. It's often easy to forget one essential part of your life; your 'you' time. The time you spend not worried about work, not focused on others, not concerned about tomorrow, not stressed about all you have to do or not do; you need to spend some time on YOU! Easiest way to lose balance is to lose sight of you!

Enemy of the Ninja

Lack of focus and distraction will destroy you, young warrior. Your ability to maintain your focus on the task at hand will directly impact your results. Focus is the cornerstone of all achievement. Zero in on your target and let nothing pull you away! Keep noise away. De-clutter! One thing at a time, one goal to be achieved. Focus, or the battle is lost.

Ninja Explains BALANCE

Ninja, this is a two-step process. The first part of the process usually lends itself to making the second part way easier. The first part of this is to decide where you are is where you will be. Class is class time. Work is work time. Family is family time. Friends are friend time. Homework is homework time. In a world where we are always accessible by phone, text, email, facebook, internet, and beyond, it's hard not to mix all of this up. Especially when a lot of the times our classes are filled with our friends, time off is filled with work to do, and personal time is hard to commit to when being tugged by everyone else; but you must do what you can to say to yourself, paper now, friends later. Family now, homework later; and they don't distract one another. Step two, having enough time for each. You'll find that if you are effective at keeping them separate, the time you've spent on each is much more worthwhile, and in that, you will find that you've got plenty of time for all things.

Ninja One Touch Knock Out Power Move
Lockdown! That's right. We're talking solitary confinement, Ninja. Keeping work and play separate does not mean starting a paper and after 20 minutes, mingling with your friends for 10 minutes, then going back to your paper for 15 and on and on with the pattern. You'll enjoy life more if you sit down, complete the paper, then you can have focused time for other things.

Ninja in Training Challenge
Train yourself to eliminate worry. Worry doesn't serve you, it doesn't get anything done, and it takes away your focus.

To ensure your full ability to balance your life and ensure that you are using time effectively, be fully engaged in what you're doing.

Ninja's Sleep

"Take rest, the field that has rested gives bountiful crop."
Ninja Ovid

Ninja Philosophy

- A sleepy ninja is a sloppy ninja
- A tired ninja is a temperamental ninja
- Nothing can replace the power of sleep

The ninja sleeps with their eyes open so as to always be ready for whatever comes; and when they wake up, they shoot lightning from their eyes. It's just how they roll. But only well rested ninjas can conjure up the power to shoot lightning from their eyes. Caught off guard and without rest, the, at one time effective and efficient ninja will transform into a drooping, dragging lump of a ninja. A rolling stone gathers no moss; but a lump ninja...let's just say the moss is gathered.

The recommended sleep dose is seven hours a night; in college, kiss the recommendation good bye. But do your best to be consistent.

Ninja Shadow Master Secret
Here's a tip, learn the art of power naps and use them frequently. A power nap can be your greatest ally in the war on sleep deprivation and feeling tired. They are great between classes and for 10 minute study breaks.

Enemy of the Ninja

The more effective you are at managing your time, getting things done, and working smart, the more time you will save, the more easily you will sleep and the better rested you will be for the challenges ahead of you.

Spend your awake time wisely. Studying for 30 minutes a day, every day before the test will enable you to study a little bit before the test, sleep well and be more effective in the test. Not studying at all until the night before the test will suck you dry and make you a piece of crap for the test. You choose what you want.

 Ninja Explains SLEEP

There is a huge disconnect between our culture and scientific study. Culturally, you've heard about successful ninjas who do everything they can, sleep as little as possible and are successful because of burning the midnight oil and getting 4 hours of rest a night. Scientifically, it's been proven time and time and time again that effectiveness, well-being, and better health are tied directly to a well-rested individual. So there's a battle; what do you do? What's right for you? One ninja can be extremely effective on 5 hours of sleep a night. Another ninja can be just as effective on 8. Both can be extremely successful. It's all in how your body operates. Listen to your body, it will guide you. Sleep when you need sleep, wake when you need to wake. One thing is for sure, however, it's not a badge of honor that you can survive on four hours of sleep. We don't care. Get what you need.

Ninja One Touch Knock Out Power Move
As difficult as it sounds, maintain some kind of regular sleep even if all it means is going to bed at the same time every night. Maybe going to bed at 9:00pm every night means you have to wake up at 12:00am to get homework done; yup, it's better than nothing being regular.

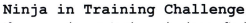

Ninja in Training Challenge
If you can't get it through sleep, find ways to give yourself more energy. Exercise, laughing, engaging in a hobby, eating right and Vitamin D are all ways that will allow you to feel more alert, upbeat and motivated.. Don't, however, depend on melatonin to fall asleep and caffeine to wake up. Developing a dependency on drugs to normalize sleep causes more harm than good.

REFLECTIONS FROM A DOJO MASTER

Hello, young grasshopper. You come seeking wisdom and guidance, it shall be rewarded.

When President Bill Clinton was in office, he was known for a couple of things (some better than others). One of the primary things Ninja President (yeah...ninja president...that's intense) Clinton was renowned for was his ability to put in long hours and get very little sleep. 4-6 hours a night, and then solve the world's problems the next day.

There are several different very successful individuals who will tell you that you don't need 7-8 hours of sleep. That you can train your body to only need 4-6 and in doing that, you can have up to 14-20 more hours a week over the average person.

The ninjas and I disagree.

Clinton may have been able to do this, but his health was not the best. In fact, after a couple years of Ninja Clinton's presidency, he was diagnosed with major heart complications without any serious signs of heart conditions or a family history of it. Ultimately this ailment was contributed to by the demands he put on his body without the powerful healing that only comes from rest.

You can challenge yourself to cut down the hours, but be smart when it comes to sleep. The more of it you have, the less stress you endure, the more effective you are during the day, your communication skills are sharper, your retention rates are higher and you have an overall better quality of life.

To your success, grasshopper.

Ninja's Struggle

Sometimes life's Hell. But hey! Whatever gets the marshmallows toasty.

Ninja J. Andrew Helt

Ninja Philosophy

- Any programs that sells you *Fast, Easy, Secrets to the Successful Ninja* for 5 easy payments of $19.95 are lying. Nothing worth doing is fast and easy.
- You get the good with the bad; the ying with the yang
- A calf is cute but nature's not sentimental; a polar bear would eat a calf

Ninja knows no fear; even in the face of defeat, danger, anguish, and adversity. For real, Ninja, problems will come at you that you can't even begin to imagine, and you'll have a choice to battle through like the ninja you are or not.

Adversity is a part of growth. With each new encounter that you succeed through, you are that much more equipped for the next challenge to come. Embrace difficulty.

> ### Ninja Shadow Master Secret
> Prepare for battle. The best thing you can do for yourself young ninja is to prepare. Struggle will come; it's inevitable on your journey to success. So the only thing you can do is continually develop yourself through positive thinking, stress management activities and proper health. PREPARE for struggle.

Enemy of the Ninja

Depression and feelings of depression occur in upwards of 80% of college students. There is a lot of challenge, pressure and new stressors that you may have never encountered. If not dealt with in a healthy way, that stress can quickly turn to despondency, sadness, hopelessness, detachment and self-doubt. If you are having these feelings, talk to people around you and do whatever you can to take the stress load piece by piece versus all at the same time. You got this ninja. Say it, "I got this." Now really loud, "I GOT THIS!"

Ninja Explains STRUGGLE

You don't get to skip the hard parts. Every successful warrior out there has had their share of struggles. There will be challenges in college socially, emotionally, physically, mentally that cannot be explained because to each individual, they will come differently; but know that as each of these challenges passes, you will survive, you will make it, and the adversity you feel now will all be put into perspective sometime down the road of life. And get ready, because the minute one challenge leaves, a new one will rear it's beast of a head. Just get ready to enjoy each day as a step towards your goals no matter what that day may present.

Ninja One Touch Knock Out Power Move
A goal you must maintain in life is to ==gain traction== daily. You must accomplish something daily as it's the easiest way to overcome overwhelming feelings. Yup, you read it right, instead of talking about how much you have to do, actually do some of what you have to do. Even if it's just writing the first paragraph of a paper- at least you did something.

Ninja in Training Challenge
Change your state. Start realizing that you must be wholly engaged in LIFE! Intellectually, emotionally, physically. All three of these parts are a part of you.

Don't get dragged down because of your physical, emotional or intellectual self is dragging! Pick yourself up by balancing them amongst each other to move yourself forward healthy and lively.

REFLECTIONS FROM A DOJO MASTER

Hello, young grasshopper. You come seeking wisdom and guidance, it shall be rewarded.

Forgive us as we go back on something we've stated in regards to not complaining. But in all fairness, things get hard, very hard and sometimes the easiest thing to do is complain. Complain!

I want you to literally pull out a sheet of paper and on it write, 'License to Complain' and pick a number under ten. Write down this phrase, inserting the number. 'For # minutes. Freely and without judgment. I do not ask you to feed my fire, but to simply allow some space'. Now fold that up and never let it leave your side.

Here are the rules: you can pull this license out only twice a day. Bearer of the license has the right to utilize all and any forms of complaining including but not limited to venting, spilling, whining, blaming, accusing, protesting, grumbling, carping, nitpicking and et cetera for up and until the extent of time in which the license allows. Immediately after time finishes, any audience given to said bearer must ask, "Great, now what?" Wherein the bearer must be solution oriented and take appropriate steps towards remedying the circumstance, situation, results and/or consequences.

To your success, grasshopper.

Ninja's Money

If you want to learn the true value of money;   lend it to someone that will not pay you back.
Ninja Mom

Ninja Philosophy
- **Ninjas understand that lending money is not smart, it's the same as giving it away.**
- **Ninja is like an eagle and watches where everything goes and comes**
- **PUNCH CREDIT CARD DEBT IN THE FACE! RIGHT IN THE FACE!**

Money can sting like the bee but it can also liberate the chained beast. Money can be your enemy; but to a ninja, it is our ally. Money means a lot of good things. Stronger nun chucks, better swords, more opportunity to fly, spin kick and hang out with your friends, or be alone in the woods...whatever your ninja fancy is.

Educate yourself in financial literacy.

> ### Ninja Shadow Master Secret
> Most colleges offer some form of a financial planning or financial management speaker, event, workshop or otherwise; GO TO THEM! GO TO AS MANY AS YOU CAN! You will never get enough money tips, education and guidance. See your financial education as an unending glass that you must always fill.

Enemy of the Ninja

The easiest way to lose your share of the castles bounty, ninja, is by not paying attention. The only one responsible for your money is you! Don't play catch up on financial planning. It's easier to stay ahead than it is to dig yourself out of the hole. Financial demands never ever stop. They never will. Be responsible for what you have. Pay attention ninja, like a shepherd watches his flock; know all that you have, all that you spend, and all that you gain. Pay attention! Pay attention! And ensure you set yourself up with a BUDGET!

 **Ninja Explains MONEY**

Anyone that tells you money isn't important knows nothing about money. Money isn't everything; but it sure helps. Students drop out of college all the time because of financial struggles; and adults drop out of life all the time because of financial struggles. The financial demands of life never go away, and you cannot place 'good intentions' into an envelope to your credit card or electricity provider. It's true, money is important. Eventually you'll have a family, you'll have a personal life, you'll want certain luxuries that can be as little as visiting family when you can, not feeling guilty about going out for dinner, or maybe an unexpected car tire will need to be replaced; these are real costs that are afforded financially. Want to know the funny thing? College is actually the time in your life where money is the least stressful. It's the time for you to learn before you get into the real world.

Ninja One Touch **Knock Out** Power Move

Don't be embarrassed if you cannot afford something. Forever, you'll have friends that want to grab a coffee, a drink, lunch, go to a concert, bowling, et cetera, and they are all good. They're not bad things, and your friends aren't bad either. You have to stick to your budget and there is no shame in saying no.

 ### Ninja in Training Challenge

First, embrace the fact that money is important. It is. Second, Practice self-control. Self-control means saving money. Saving money means not touching it. Take at least 10% of everything you earn ever and SAVE IT. Practice self-control.

Ninja's Manage Emotions

A man who is master of himself can end a sorrow as easily as he can invent a pleasure.
I don't want to be at the mercy of my emotions.
I want to use them, to enjoy them, and to dominate them.

Ninja Oscar Wilde

Ninja Philosophy

- **Be like nice kitty when necessary; be like flipped-out angry kitty when necessary – both you choose at the necessary time**

Ninja, you are like a cyclone; and cyclones get power from the heart of a calm and tempered center. .

> ### Ninja Shadow Master Secret
> Breathe and walk. The best thing you can do for yourself when needing to collect your emotions is to go for a 15 minute walk (alone). 15 minutes is all it takes to change your state, release initial feelings, and gather yourself for the next steps to progress through emotions.

Enemy of the Ninja

Angry tiger alert! High emotion often equates to low intelligence. When we are in high states of emotion, we do and say things we wouldn't say or do when we are in a collected state of openness, collectedness and responsiveness. When a tiger is cornered, he will lash out irrationally in order to survive, even if that means doing damage to itself. Ninjas do that too when they are at high levels of emotion: fear, scarcity, insecurity, anger, frustration, sadness, even over happiness, excitement or other. When tigers have high energy, they do dumb things; when we are in high energy, we do dumb things. Breathe and collect yourself, don't let your emotions take you into a direction you will regret tomorrow.

Ninja Explains MANGE EMOTIONS

Many college ninjas shut down when emotion gets to them. The stress is overwhelming, the relationships are too drama-centered, the losing football game is the last thread of hope now gone, the demands of work, family, grades, friends is enough to make you flip out and snap. The most successful ninjas in college are the ones that understand their triggers, they understand what instances lead to what emotions, and they also understand what actions they need to take when faced with certain emotions. When feeling sad, what do you need to do to move forward? When angry, what needs to happen to collect yourself? When tired, what must you do to feel enlivened? Each emotion of yours is just like a padlock; each emotion has a specific combination that must be used in order to release the bondage that can come from being controlled by your emotions. Embrace your feelings, but at the same time, master the combinations for each so that you are in control not controlled.

Ninja One Touch Knock Out Power Move

Never write an email or text out of reactive emotions. Sometimes challenges are communicated, feedback is given or obstacles are presented through non conversational formats, and sometimes, these messages will rile you up. Breathe, sleep on it, and don't respond until you're clearly thinking.

Ninja in Training Challenge

Be continuously aware of how you respond and how you react to stimuli. When you react, you can be impulsive and end up in more trouble than you need. The best thing to do is respond, rationally, logically, and after letting the initial emotions go. Notice that when you respond, the outcomes are better, you feel better, and there are a lot less regrets.

Quick Tip

Journaling has about 30+ solid benefits! Journals are used as an intentional review of things, events, and plans and SIGNIFICANTLY HELP IN IDENFITYING YOUR emotional triggers and responses.

Did you know that dedicating 15-30 minutes of journaling everyday can reduce stress, increase focus, create stability, improve organization skills, clear your mind, promote self-therapy, detach you from regret or other negative feelings, strengthen your sense of self, build personal identity and self-esteem, create awareness, ease decision making, and increase your memory! WOW! Give someone a high five and say **THAT'S A LOT FOR ONLY 15-30 MINUTES!** So put the stress and worry to the side, and empty your mind by filling a page! For the next 7 days, take the action of JOURNALING for 15-30 minutes, and reflect for yourself how this simple action will move you forward and help your growth.

The BEST template you can use is this: Three columns.
One is THE EVENT. Two is WHAT I DID. Three is THE RESULT AND MY FEELING.

You'll find that after FOUR YEARS OF DOING THIS, you'll have built yourself an ENCYCLOPEDIA, A ROAD MAP, A PERFECT PERSONAL GUIDE for how you should handle any situation, environment, feeling or obstacle!

Ninja's Keep it Clean

Organizing is what you do before you do something,
so that when you do it, it is not all mixed up.

Ninja A. A. Milne

Ninja Philosophy

- o **Notes and studies organized means your studies are in order**
- o **Get all that down, life organization is hella awesome**

Have you ever seen an uncollected or disheveled or untidy ninja? No way! They are collected, together, all in one, compact. Ninjas are like Swiss Army Pocket Knives; they have everything they need right in place, all compacted in one cool looking red handle, and when they are done using one of the tools, they put it back and pull out the other.

Get your crap in order; how you keep your environment says a lot about you as a person.

> ### Ninja Shadow Master Secret
> Get a planner where you can keep all your plans, due dates, test dates, event dates, date dates, interviews, schedules, appointments and otherwise. If you don't, you'll miss something!

Enemy of the Ninja

Clutter and chaos and mess are not keys to success; in fact they are the opposite. They cause stress, ineffectiveness and distraction. Keep your stress low and your living space at a presentable standard. If this is too much to ask; at a minimum, maintain your study space! Your study space will be where you go to get the main goal accomplished; and that goal is the best you can possibly be for your academic success which will lead to career success. Keep your work/study space put together and in order.

Ninja Explains KEEP IT CLEAN

You don't live at home anymore; you're on your own. Laundry needs to get done and you are the one that's going to do it. Dishes need to be clean, guess who is getting them done. Garbage taken out, that's all you too. If you have bills; those are yours to pay! You need to be on time for the things that have a set start time. All things must be maintained, cleaned and organized by you; that's how it is! Choose to be a person that's organized, that's together, that's collected and not scattered, that's on time, that presents a great first impression through how they show up professionally, personally, as an individual through your living, work, and travel space.

Ninja One Touch Knock Out Power Move
No pets in college! That's flippin right! No pets in college! "But I want a fish/lizard/turtle/bird/kitten/hamster...et cetera." DON'T GET AN ANIMAL! They cost you more stress, time and resources that you don't have to give.

Ninja in Training Challenge
Sometimes success in college and in life means doing things because you must, not because you want to.

As hard as it may be to see the connection between keeping your stuff in order to help maintain the order of your life; there is a connection. A big one. Develop the habits of organization now so that they are available for you in your career. Employers don't like unorganized employees.

Ninja Words You Should Know

Seishin-teki kyōyō (spiritual refinement)

- **Taijutsu** (unarmed combat, using one's body as the only weapon)
- **Kenjutsu** (sword fighting)
- **Bōjutsu** (stick and staff fighting)
- **Shurikenjutsu** (throwing blades)
- **Sōjutsu** (spear fighting)
- **Naginatajutsu** (naginata fighting)
- **Sui-ren** (water training)
- **Bōryaku** (tactic)
- **Chōhō** (espionage)
- **Intonjutsu** (escaping and concealment)
- **Hensōjutsu** (disguise & impersonation)
- **Shinobi-iri** (stealth and entering methods)
- **Bajutsu** (horsemanship)
- **Grappling Hook (**A three or four pronged tool for awesomeness that is tied to a very very very long rope or cord. It's the only thing you'll ever need (in addition to this book) for success and the sheer reason of saying, "I have a grappling hook, would you like to see it?" **Not only is this the perfect ice-breaker for introducing yourself to a member of the opposite sex,** but it's also the best way to create awe. In addition, you can scale tall buildings or walls if for any reason you ever need to do that. Like if the library is closed but you just need to get in.)
- **Trail Mix** (The greatest thing ever invented after grappling hooks. I could eat it every day for the rest of my life. It comes in several flavors and, similar to chili, it includes a variety of ingredients. In fact, just like chili, you can dump just about anything in there and it'll be awesome. The only thing different from chili, come to think of it, is that trail mix is dry whereas chili is wet.)
- **Trail-Mix-utsu-seishin-teki-kyōyō-grappling-hook-topofbuilding-hhōhō** (The art of finding spiritual fulfillment through the making trail mix while spying atop a building that was scaled by using your grappling hook. Basically, utopia; also known as euphoria or rapture.)
- **College-utsu** (ninjaing the hell out of college)
- **College-trail-mix-bajutsu** (ninjaing the hell out of college while eating trail mix and riding a horse)
- **No-One-Can-Say-No-Or-Yes-If-You-Never-Askutsu** (if you are so inclined, please send trail mix to the author of this book)

STUDY, STRIKE, SUCCEED

Ninja, get this done with the reflection of a lake.

What triggers most of my stress?

_____

_____

_____

I have a tendency to say 'should' a lot. I should study more. I should eat right. I should make my bed. What are the biggest should that you know need to start happening now?

_____

_____

_____

What preventative measures can I take to deter/lessen stress (examples include keep a clean room, exercise, me time, et cetera)?

_____

_____

What's my me-time, secret ninja relax and reflect plan?
How much time a day? _____

Where? _____

Music or not? And what kind? _____

When? _____

What am I doing? _____

What's around me/in the environment? _____

Outside or in? _____

Other: _____

What are the major distractors in my life that keep me off target and off plan?

What can I do to help lessen the impact of distractors from my world?

The following things energize me and put some spirit back into my step:

Are their money courses, speakers, workshops offered by your campus?

When are they, where are they?

I hereby state that I will do whatever it takes to attend a financial education opportunity so I can be one rock star money ninja!

Signature:

Do the people I live with share my values on health, eating, exercise and cleanliness? How is that impacting our emotional wellbeing?

Journal Template as Mentioned in Previous Section. Note the space available. This isn't meant as a dear diary, this is for quick snap shots of activities, responses and outcomes so that you can see where you are and where you want to be quickly.

	THE EVENT	WHAT I DID	RESULT/MY FEELING
Monday			
Tuesday			
Wednesday			
Thursday			
Friday			
Saturday			
Sunday			

Personal Notes from This Section

_____
_____
_____
_____
_____
_____
_____
_____
_____
_____
_____
_____
_____
_____
_____
_____
_____
_____

Questions I still Have

_____
_____
_____
_____
_____
_____

How I intend to get answers

_____
_____
_____

Things I want to discuss with a professor, mentor, or advisor.

To improve in my ninja skills and to better my abilities of becoming an ultimate success ninja, I will take it upon myself to follow through on the following discipline/commitment/action each day this week:

I understand that it may not be easy, it may be a little different, but if I'm to truly master the art of nin, then let the above statement be burned in steal by the dragon of a thousand daggers. I will complete by the end of the week.

Third Skill Set

Build a Supportive Social Life

People don't know what they don't know. I say that sparingly and with definite purpose because I can talk about this next topic until I'm blue in the face and 99% of students would say to me, "Yup, I know that." But knowing is one thing, understanding is another.

It's hard to see the picture when you're in the frame. It's hard to see how you can transform when every day you change just a little, one day at a time.

The people you spend the most time with have greater impact on your health than the foods you eat, the sleep you get, and the exercise you do. Seriously! There are reports on this stuff! You can be the most confident, independent, socially aware and stubborn in who you are, but if you spend the right amount of time with the right or wrong people, you'll become them. You will take on their language patterns, their tempers, their conversation style, their health habits, the way they treat others and the way they treat themselves. This means, quite literally, there are some people that you just cannot afford to spend a lot of time with, and some of these people will be your friends, roommates, or otherwise. At the same time, there are some people you should find out how you can spend more time with!

You should be strategic about the social network you commit yourself to Student organizations, leadership initiatives, volunteer work, social events sponsored by your res halls are all places to meet people that will build you up, hold you to standards, and push you to be more.

A Ninja's Friends

Tell me thy company, and I'll tell thee what thou art.

Ninja Don Quixote

Ninja Philosophy

- Some say friends; ninjas say right arm
- A ninja is an island; an island full of ninjas is way better
- Know thyself, know thy goals, know thy friends is what thy becomes

Ninja, alone in the shadows, stalking, spying, striking, you know you are effective; but wouldn't it be nice to have some peeps around? Independence is an awesome power that will allow you to accomplish great things; but when you can influence a pack and be part of a group that shares that goal of taking down an elephant, you can multiply your abilities by a million and a half.

The people you surround yourself with play more of a role on your health than the food you eat or the exercise you participate in.

Ninja Shadow Master Secret

Get in an active habit of introducing yourself. Don't walk around with your eyes on the ground, put some spring in your step, a smile on your face, and say hello to everyone you meet. This will help you expand your network, but also help you in your confidence, emotional management, and communication skills.

Enemy of the Ninja

Fear of Rejection. A ninja knows no fear. Don't take rejection personally. Start taking every little thing personal and all of a sudden you're going to think there is something wrong with you. There is nothing wrong with you; there's nothing wrong with others. I'm okay, you're okay, everyone is okay. We have differences and some people will not click with you; it's none of your business why they don't, some people just won't. Be okay with it. You've done nothing wrong; continue to put yourself out there. The right people will eventually be in your world.

Ninja Explains FRIENDS

You must have a social life, ninja. Let me rephrase, you must have a healthy social life. You are the average of the five people you spend the most time with.

Take a look at the habits of those around you, don't judge them; but ask yourself if their habits and lifestyles are the habits and lifestyle that you want. From social habits and study habits to spending and exercise habits, all of these aspects of your life will be impacted by those you surround yourself with. Lastly, whoever you are around, there is one thing you must be able to do and that is to be completely and 100% yourself without feeling threatened, pressured or out of place. Find people that will support and challenge you. People that you can trust and learn from; avoid people that will insult, gossip and take away your sense of pride and self.

Ninja One Touch Knock Out Power Move

Start a mastermind group and meet monthly. This group should be a group of individuals/friends that share the same passions and interests where you can meet monthly to talk about ideas, opportunities and share insight and collaboration. They are awesome for energy and momentum towards starting businesses or accomplishing goals!

Ninja in Training Challenge

Watch carefully the people you are attracting to your life. Do they infect others with mediocrity or are they affecting others with greatness and a positive attitude?

O of the hardest things you'll ever have to do is say good bye to someone that may be harming you; but remember, when one door closes, two will open in its place.

Reflections from a Dojo Master

Hello, young grasshopper. You come seeking
wisdom and guidance, it shall be rewarded.

People have asked me, "How do I manage peer pressure? How am I
supposed to develop the confidence and ability to not feel like I have to do
something?"

I get that question a lot because managing peer pressure is a lot harder than
just saying to yourself that you know what's right and what's wrong. The
most effective way I've ever helped people overcome peer pressure has been
through a process that seems really weird and really uncomfortable, but
ultimately, this exercise has proven results.

If you want to develop your ability to manage peer pressure, take one day
every three weeks (or more often if you'd like), and go be sold to! Literally,
go intentionally seek out opportunities where people will try to sell you
something. The emotion, behaviors and techniques involved in sales are the
exact same as the emotion, behaviors and techniques experienced in peer
pressure situations.

Go to cell phone kiosks in the mall, go to car dealerships, call credit card
companies (all with the mentality that you will say NO! Regardless, you will
say NO! It's an experiment not a want to buy.) and go get sold to and observe
how you respond, learn what helps you feel comfortable saying NO, and
develop your ability to stand your ground.

To your success, grasshopper.

A Ninja's Love Interests

I present myself to you in a form suitable to the relationship I wish to achieve with you.

Ninja Luigi Pirandello

Ninja Philosophy

- The easiest way to confuse a ninja is to pull at their heart strings
- The easiest way to find comfort is through a person that respects your heart strings

Sigh ninja, the faint linger of love and also the rusty sharp pain of love, both will knock at your door, will you answer their calls? The manipulative and overwhelming and awesome perplexity of romantic relationships will kick your butt. It can distract, enchant, take your focus off the goal, keep you up at night, make your head spin, make you feel on top of the world, fulfilled, dead, alive, good, bad, healthy, and sick all at the same time. Unfortunately for you, all that stuff associated with love, doesn't happen in a set order; instead, it usually happens all at once so that it can be as confusing and as difficult as possible.

Are you excited about dating yet? All I'm saying is know how to stand on your own two feet with a sense of pride and self-respect. That's all.

Ninja Shadow Master Secret

Develop your sense of who you are, your values and your ability to be alone before entering into a relationship. Relationships can be wonderful when no one is confused about who they are as an individual before they identify themselves by another person.

Enemy of the Ninja

The NEED for a relationship is a terrible lie you tell yourself. It starts in your brain, travels to the heart, then to your motivation, your sense of self-worth and eventually your grades. You don't NEED to be in a relationship. You don't NEED to be in love. You don't NEED to define who you are by your dating habits! You NEED to be happy with you. You NEED to be confident in you. You NEED to know that it will all make sense eventually.

☷ Ninja Explains LOVE

College can sometimes feel like the Meat Market where everyone just wants to show off their best cut of meat and have you buy their goods (no pun intended). Don't allow love to be your number one focus in life because it can significantly impact your grades, health and wellbeing; and if you are at school just to meet the love of your life, there are a lot of cheaper alternatives that are way more effective. Let's get to the nitty-gritty; having a companion you can share everything with is beneficial, but not as necessary as air. High school relationships succeed less than 5% of the time. If he/she asks you to spend less time with friends or cuts you off from them, that's a no go. If your significant other is crazy, chances are you can't save them or fix them or change them. Jealousy isn't cute. Respect is awesome. Compromise is necessary and love and sex are two different things. Take that NINJA!

Ninja One Touch Knock Out Power Move
If they are asking you, "what do you see in that person?" And your response is, "you don't know what it's like when we're alone," or, "he/she used to be___." It's time to leave that relationship.

Ninja in Training Challenge
Trust and mutual respect are the keys to a relationship. Ninja, you're sly with your language, it's tricky. So tricky, in fact, that it can often be used to trick yourself. Be honest with yourself in a relationship. Be honest if your relationship is healthy, respectful and trustworthy; don't justify the negative aspects. There are negative parts to everything; don't be naïve about it.

NINJA DOESN'T PARTY; NINJA IS THE PARTY

"It increases the desire, but it takes away the (academic)-performance."
Ninja William Shakespeare

NINJA PHILOSOPHY

- Ninja knows how to go to a party, ninja knows how to leave a party on their terms, when they want to, in the way they want
- If a party is uncomfortable feeling, ninja knows to disappear

Ninja, party is a two headed beast. One head of the party scene is one in which clouds, tricks and black magic thoughts will toil and turn; the other it is one in which you can meet people, get out of the dorm, and have fun. Both exist, you must be the master of which you battle. No matter what the situation, always bring a trusted friend, a bottle of water, and a phone to be used if you need a ride home, not to text your ex.

You don't need to party to have fun. You don't need to drink if you're at a party. You do need to meet people that will support your choices, your boundaries and you.

> ### Ninja Shadow Master Secret
> Moderation and self-control. Chances are, this book won't sway you from getting drunk; but take that as a hint. If you and 1000 others are reading this, you could be the one out of a thousand that says, "I am the true ninja. People enjoy me apart from when I drink. And I'm graduating in four years because my homework is done before I drink, not after."

Enemy of the Ninja

Alcohol abuse, peer pressure, sexual misconduct, and poor choice making are all tied to the college party scene. This isn't a scare tactic; this is honest. From one ninja to another, drama and baggage accompany college parties 99.97% of the time; drama and baggage that you're better off without.

 **Ninja Explains PARTY**

Yes, you are in college, you have some independence, and you have access to alcohol, parties and reckless behavior, which can lead to hospitalization, dropping out of school, pregnancy, STDs, legal fines and academic trouble. Have you ever heard of a ninja that drank too little and that's why they got in trouble? You can maintain your coolness and your sense of pride even if you don't party. As funny as it seems, it's not funny that you may not be able to remember what happened last night. It's not hilarious that you don't know where you are or who you're with, and the story about the one time you were with a bunch of your buddies and (fill in the blank) will not ever be something you share with future friends or employers in order to earn street-credit.

Ninja One Touch Knock Out Power Move
One in four women are survivors of sexual violence while in college. Every party, every bar, bring someone you know, you trust, and that you can depend on to keep a level head if you plan on tilting yours for the evening.

 Ninja in Training Challenge
Did you know that if you stay drunk all weekend, you can lose up to 30% of what you learned the week before. Your studies should be the priority over the parties.

There will always be another party; their might not always be the opportunity to raise your GPA.

REFLECTIONS FROM A DOJO MASTER

Hello, young grasshopper. You come seeking
wisdom and guidance, it shall be rewarded.

I saw an interview with Master Ninja Donald Trump (you know...the billionaire guy with a lot of property, money, high cheek bones, and owner of the universe). Donald Trump drilled one point in his interview about how he became as successful as he did.

"What's one thing you learned or lesson you'd share with people that will dramatically impact their business and results?"

Trump responded, "What my dad taught me. Don't drink. Don't smoke. Period. Don't drink. Don't smoke. Don't drink. Don't smoke." Those were his exact words. "I never drank, I never smoked. Ever. That's it. People get caught up in this stuff and they can't function, they don't work, they waste. Don't drink. Don't smoke." He continued, "People ask me, 'You don't drink? That must be difficult.' No! It's not. It's a choice. I don't do it."

Young ninja, I understand that the party-scene is an appealing part of college. That it acts as almost a cornerstone to the college experience, and that the wild stories of people are appealing and fanciful; here's the bottom line, it's not worth it. It's not worth the wasted time, money, energy and DRAMA. It's not worth feeling like crap the next day, it's not worth the apologies for the drunk text messages you make, and it's not worth the fleeting, momentary, temporary rock star-like feeling. Every person I've EVER talked to...seriously EVER talked to...offers me a list of negative outcomes that is always three times as long as the list of positive outcomes from a night of drinking.

There's no glory, greatness or triumph in being the person that can 'hold his own'. There's a lot more to be said for the person that stands on their convictions, is confident in their decisions, and has the willpower to say 'no'. Do you have any idea how attractive that kind of confidence is to the opposite sex? A LOT MORE than the person on the floor that can't even hold a conversation without half way passing out.

From Ninja Master Owner of the Universe Donald Trump, "Don't drink. Don't smoke."

To your success, grasshopper.

Ninja's Sex

Love is the answer, but while you are waiting for the answer,
sex raises some pretty good questions.

Ninja Woody Allen

Ninja Philosophy

- o **Casual sex is not ninja approved and feels empty in the end**
- o **If someone says they feel rejected because ninja won't sleep with them; it's time ninja reevaluates the relationship**
- o **Sex doesn't increase your chances of a healthy long-term relationship**
- o **When in doubt, Ninja, say NO**

Now, aside from the fact that ninja sex sounds awesome; there's more to it than just sex. It's never just sex; baggage, drama, emotion, feelings, sometimes manipulation, consequences, or new responsibility come with it. Don't let the sneaky monkeys convince you that it's "cool-no strings attached," there are always strings. Those strings are always attached.

Never harden yourself to the idea that sex isn't an emotional or intimate thing. It always is and always will be. So don't just go showing off to everyone how you use your ninja weaponry.

Ninja Shadow Master Secret
Seriously, don't joke around on this one. Rule of thumb; if you aren't ready to have a child, you're not ready to have sex. If you want to be respected by your peers, you don't give it away. If you feel pressured, don't act like it was a clear choice. Sex. As much as some of us have numbed ourselves to its specialness, it's still a powerful emotional choice.

Enemy of the Ninja

Whatever. It's not a big deal. It's just one time. I don't really care. It didn't mean anything. The list goes on and on here. Validating or rationalizing your choice doesn't take away the fact that you engaged in an intimate and emotional bond with another person. Being in an environment where you feel pressured to have sex, and your ninja intuition is uncertain and is in an epic battle against "It's not that big of a deal," is a red flag that it's time to be a stronger you and find someone that understands that sex isn't just sex, and that it is a big deal, it is a mature choice, and that you should really care.

 Ninja Explains SEX

Respect yourself. Respect your body. Respect who you are, what you stand for and what you're all about. Sex shouldn't be a subject of objectivity; it used to be thought of as the one true and most intimate thing to share with a person. Why? Because – true story – when you engage in sex with another person, your body releases chemicals that you cannot stop. These chemicals cause the brain to focus on long-term commitment and protective instincts towards the other person. In our world where sex is marketed, commercialized, available, and accessible; it's harder to stick to saying no.

Ninja One Touch Knock Out Power Move
70% of College Students fall through on a personal commitment to themselves to not engage in sex while in college; mostly due to circumstances that involved alcohol or peer pressure. Don't choose to engage in sex if you are under the influence. Drunk does not make for healthy choices.

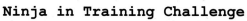

Ninja in Training Challenge

Ninja say educate thyself. Most people know one thing about sex: it can make a child. THERE'S A LOT MORE THAT GOES INTO IT! Chemicals are released, emotions are involved, psychology creates an understanding and messaging, and relationship development. It's beyond physical! Have you and your partner been able to have a mature conversation about it? Have you set realistic expectations of what it means to you? What does sex mean to you? Are you aware of the risks and consequences? Do you know all that you should and

Ninja's Open Communication

"Communication is not only the essence of being human, but also a vital property of life."
Ninja John A. Piece

Ninja Philosophy

- **Think before you speak; you cannot un-speak what's been spoken**
- **If ninja harbors inner feelings without sharing, unrest happens and consumes ninja like a fire in town of straw**

People want information FAST and they want to UNDERSTAND WHAT YOUR POINT IS. The world wants CLEAR, direct and concise information. So if you aren't fast and you aren't pointed and you're not clear like cellophane when you communicate...time to practice.

Ninja Shadow Master Secret

Seeking: Candidate with effective communication skills. That's all over the place for possible job opportunities. Employers want ninjas that can get to the point of what they want to say clearly, effectively and with unwavering confidence. Begin to be conscious of how you talk; do you beat around the bush, are you too vague, are you unsure? What is the message you are really conveying?

Enemy of the Ninja

Half truthing is as bad as not trothing. If you are a ninja that wants the respect and alliance of others, be the ninja that leaves nothing out of the story and has all their cards on the table. If someone asks you their opinion, share your full opinion. If you are uncertain about an explanation; say you're uncertain. If you are telling a story or giving an answer; don't leave out things because you want your audience to assume more or less than what actually happened. Tell the full truth, the whole story, morning glory.

Ninja Explains Open Communication

Ninja, say what's on your mind. Say what you need to say and be open to the sayings of others. Too many people are timid when it comes to sharing and being open with the things that need to be said; and that's why there is so much drama in our world and in our college careers; it's also why so many of us just go wherever the wind blows because we don't want to cause discomfort or have the tough conversations. Honest, clear, and concise communication is essential to lasting relationships. If you aren't transparent with your words and your words don't reflect what's on your mind; much regret and 'wishing you would have' will come your way. You may not be the professional in a topic, but you're still the professional of you. Eliminate drama and address your challenges with others forwardly. Strengthen relationships and share your appreciation with others. Make sure you're conscious is clear and ask what needs to be asked. You must also learn the value in listening and hearing others respectfully and without bias.

Ninja One Touch Knock Out Power Move
Begin to ask more questions, it's the best way to create dialogue, understanding, trust and open communication. You should always ask questions: in class, with friends, in groups, to your career counselor, in your clubs, at work, in meetings, at interviews. Questions are a sign of an intelligent, insightful, critical thinking. ASK ASK ASK!

Ninja in Training Challenge

Practice talking. Sounds crazy because if you're in college, chances are you can talk; but this is actually a practice that successful people have done for years.

Need to make an important phone call to follow up about a resume? Practice first. Having a meeting with a mentor? Write down the questions and practice first. Going to a networking event? Practice introducing yourself.

 ## REFLECTIONS FROM A DOJO MASTER

Challenges with other people. You will have them. In group settings, peer networks, co-workers, employers, and beyond. If you want those challenges to come to an end sooner rather than later, DO NOT look to other people to solve the problems. Go to the source!

Gossip and drama and distrust is created if you choose to speak with a third party versus just having the tough conversations directly. Stop avoiding difficulty. Get to a solution by addressing the individual you have a challenge with. This is the most productive path to a solution.

Ninja's Take Nothing Personally

It's not personal, Sonny. It's strictly business.
Ninja Michael Corleone (The Godfather)

Ninja Philosophy

- Ninjas emotions get in the way of business
- To be effective with others and with oneself, one must remove angry tiger and invite in warm butterfly
- Hurt feelings have a greater chance of slowing a ninja down than a dagger to the face

Ninja master emotions. Ninjas are the eye of the storm. Ninjas are not offended by the whims and jests of others. That's useless! Ninja's don't do useless because they are too busy being effective. Since a ninja is never useless, being hurt or crabby because of some other element is never useful!

> **Ninja Shadow Master Secret**
> You are liked, you are disliked, someone likes your shirt, someone else doesn't. What does it matter. Some will, some won't, so what, there is always someone else. If you internalize either the recognition or the feedback, you'll be tied to it. Do your best to not fluff your pillow, and not beat yourself up, but to learn and move forward.

Enemy of the Ninja

Dependence on feedback, praise, recognition is like a polar bear that's dependent on the ice. What happens when it all melts away? Well, you end up all wet with no footing. A ninja does not look to the world to dive him or her forward. Some will like you, some will not like you, so what, other people are waiting to meet you! That's life! If you go through life always needing praise, do you stop when the praise stops? Or at the faintest hint of rejection do you shut down? Ninjas are known to be some of the most disciplined, confident, independent assassin warriors ever; but if there is one addiction that catches them, it's the drug of 'good job'. Don't mess with it. It's a gateway drug to a dependency of other opinions.

Ninja Explains TAKE NOTHING PERSONALLY

Get a thicker skin. Now, I'm all about being sensitive and I am the first to admit that feelings can get hurt easily and often; but you can't control what people think, just like you can't control what people say. The only thing you can control is how you respond to whatever comes your way. If you take everything personally and internalize it, ninja, my friend, you have a long, hard road ahead of you. If you take in everything, reflect on it, see it as neither good, nor bad, and let it go, your life will feel so much lighter, better and you'll be an overall happier person. An opinion about you is nothing more than a reflection of the person sharing their opinion. You can't allow your results and self-worth be dependent on others. Some people will like your new haircut, some won't. Ninja, you're above the opinions of mere mortals.

Ninja One Touch Knock Out Power Move
Every time I ever have to have a challenging conversation with a friend, group mate or family member, I always preface the conversation with, "Listen, this is purely business. It's not an attack on who you are. Let's put all of our cards on the table, say what we need to say, and figure out how we can move forward." It's not personal, it's business.

Ninja in Training Challenge

The nature of a ninja is a constant. It does not change, it does not alter, it does not lose integrity. Nin is an everlasting presence and is consistent regardless of circumstance, similar to that of rain. The nature of rain never changes, it is a constant. Rain feeds the marshes and it feeds the fields. Weeds grow in the marshes, flowers in the fields. Different results, yet the nature of rain never changes.

You will be greeted by people that have marshes for brains. Don't let how they respond to you impact how you view yourself. You are the ninja, you are constant. Remind yourself, you are the rain.

STUDY, STRIKE, SUCCEED

Ninja, get this done with the clarity of a scuba diver's mask.

What do I expect from a healthy relationship?

_____

_____

_____

_____

What should others expect from me in a healthy relationship?

_____

_____

_____

_____

If I were to develop a personal sounding board of five individuals that I could trust to take themselves emotionally out of a situation and give me an honest, non-biased opinion, those people would be:

_____

_____

_____

What benefit could I gain from forming a mastermind group?

_____

_____

_____

What characteristics of a mastermind would make me want to attend one on a weekly basis?

_____

_____

_____

Who would I invite to a mastermind? Are their people I know of that I need to get to know better in order to have them as a part of my mastermind? List five with their contact information

_____

_____

_____

When is the best time to host this mastermind group? _____

How do we handle no-shows? _____

Where and through what media channel will we connect? _____

_____

How long will our mastermind meet for? How often? _____

_____

What is the format of our discussion? Or will we use the following template?

Welcome and quick 'hi, how are yous' – 7 minutes.
First person – Update. Successes since last conversation. Challenges. Goals. Deadline for goal. – 10 minutes
Each person gives feedback, suggestions. – 2 minutes each
Repeat for persons 2-5.
Recap, thanks, talk to you next week – 5 minutes.
Personal notes and reflection from mastermind – 6 minutes

Do I ask good questions? Are they open ended or yes and no questions?

Begin a database of 'good questions' and memorize them.

Sample What did you particularly enjoy about today's presentation (as opposed to 'did you like today's presentation)?

Sample What kind of progress have you gained since last we spoke (as opposed to what's new)?

Sample What is it about this topic that particularly excites you (as opposed to do you enjoy the program)?

Sample How are you today? Good. What would it take for me to help it get to outstanding (as opposed to just how are you today)?

Relationship Assessment:

Communication

How comfortable do you feel bringing up challenges or discussions with the other person?

When talking, is there an equal sharing in the discussion? Do both people contribute, or does one person typically lead?

Trust

Is your trust expressed through confidence and support, or through going behind each other's back?

Has your partner ever given you a specific reason not to trust him/her?

_____

_____

If so, what type of discussion surrounded this to move forward and overcome this?

_____

_____

Openness/honesty

Do you feel comfortable bringing up grievance and enjoyments with your partner?

_____

_____

Do you feel comfortable being a true version of yourself around your partner? Can you be the same person you are in front of your family, friends, professors, colleagues, etc.?

_____

_____

_____

Adaptation to Change

Do you feel that you and your partner have changed well together over time and circumstances?

_____

_____

Do you feel confident that in continual change and transition you and your partner will continue to grow together?

_____

_____

Does sex mean anything to me?

_____

_____

Personal Notes from This Section

_____

_____

_____

_____

Questions I still Have

_____

_____

_____

How I intend to get answers

_____

_____

Things I want to discuss with a professor, mentor, or advisor.

_____

_____

To improve in my ninja skills and to better my abilities of becoming an ultimate success ninja, I will take it upon myself to follow through on the following discipline/commitment/action each day this week:

_____

_____

I understand that it may not be easy, it may be a little different, but if I'm to truly master the art of nin, then let the above statement be burned in steal by the dragon of a thousand daggers. I will complete by the end of the week.

Fourth Skill Set

Finding Your Feet

Floating on cloud nine or chained to uncertainty or wandering aimlessly. That's the awesome cycle they call college (and life for that matter), but that's not bad! The ups and downs and ins and outs and backwards and forwards of what is your life is what we like to call living!

Life is all about uncertainties mixed with risk and opportunity, confidence and insecurity. It's a constant duality of 'all put together' and 'complete chaos'.

College is life. Life is college. Just when you think you have it all aligned, everything falls apart. There will be a lot thrown at you that you may have never experienced before. The concepts you will learn about in this section will give you the ability to anchor yourself. In the process of your progress, it's best to be conscious of your development. You have new independence and bigger choices to make without a safety net. Handle this new independence as if it were your most valuable resource. Cherish it. Care for it. Nurture it. And if you pair it with the right attitude and unwavering confidence, not to mention the ideas presented in the next few pages, young ninja, you're on the right route.

A Ninja is an Army of One

The true character of liberty is **independence**, maintained by force.

Ninja Voltaire

Ninja Philosophy

- o Ninjas are **self-motivated;** if they aren't, they would die
- o Ninjas understand that solitude can be awesome, and it   can be destructive

Take on the world, and know that in order to take on the world, there will be times where you must get the strength, courage and motivation from none other than yourself.

People are on your side and will be by your side, but there are times where you must know you, be you, and act from within you, independently.

Ninja Shadow Master Secret
You need to develop the ability to be alone, because it's what you do when no one is looking that's important. Do you have a tough time being alone? Do you need constant social interaction? Is it hard to focus on getting things done? Are you bored, worried or anxious if no one is around? Can you motivate and be happy with you?

Enemy of the Ninja

Co-dependency is a behavioral habit that people develop through the constant need to fulfill other people's needs or a constant need to not feel abandoned. It happens, especially to new college students that aren't used to being on their own as an independent young ninja. The attention of others can be as addicting as a drug. Develop a daily routine where you take some time for you and use that time to be effective, be productive and build your independent confidence.

Ninja Explains INDEPENDENCE

College is where you really come to find who you are and what you're all about. What you do here will determine how you live and what you accomplish after, so it is important to develop a strong, healthy, disciplined sense of independence. This can be taken two ways. Some people take this new independence from the perspective of no more rules, no one to answer to, and do whatever they want to an abusive and extreme level. Others take this ==independence a==s a time to truly test their skills, abilities, attitudes and commitment to being the best they can be.

Ninja One Touch Knock Out Power Move
Find a club, organization or hobby, or go to some campus events without your typical group of friends, or better, go alone! Discover for yourself that you can enjoy yourself, meet new people, and develop a strong independence without constantly needing the comfort zone of your friends in order to make an impression or enjoy an opportunity.

Ninja in Training Challenge
Take some chances on yourself. The more you develop a sense of action and self-pride based on your own accomplishments and sense of self rather than from external sources; the more notable and confident you will be in doing what you can do based on your hopes and dreams. ==At the end of the day, the only person you have to answer to is you; remember that.== Are you doing what will make you fulfilled, proud and confident? Or are you waiting for others to come with you, or worse, going wherever they take you?

Ninja's Choices

Life is a sum of all your choices.
Ninja Albert Camus

Ninja Philosophy

- Ninjas have many tools, the choice to use them is theirs
- Nobody else is going to get a ninja to fly; it's up to ninja to fly

Life is a series of choices. It truly is. You choose the meaning you create, the value to gain., the responsibility to you take, the people you associate with, when you wake up in the morning. These things are all your choices and they all have consequences and rewards. You take the bad and the good, that's part of a ninja life.

At any moment, you are at choice and the only person that will make that choice is you.

Ninja Shadow Master Secret

Don't be a victim of circumstance. You are smart enough, you are pretty enough, you came from the right family, you came from the right economic background, and if you have the wherewithal to read this book, you have the wherewithal to take your life and make the choice to be great and accomplish the best ninja powers ever.

Enemy of the Ninja

Ninja, you are a slave to your habits. Often times it's hard to break free from the chains that imprison us to our self-taught reality. Your world is a direct product of your choices and the habits you've created. If you don't like your results in life, change your habits. It's that easy. Sometimes, the feeling of hopelessness or that 'this is just the way it is' is something to fall into; but it's just as easy to do what you normally wouldn't do until it becomes a better stronger habit for you. Just because you've told yourself you are insecure for the past 20 years, doesn't mean that you can't do something brave. Be brave, make a choice, make a change, move yourself forward to be the ninja you deserve.

Ninja Explains Choice

Choice is pretty straight forward; but not many ninjas truly understand its unlimited power. The minute you internalize the all out and true power of choice, it's like you'll see the world through a different pair of eyes. What can taking ownership of your choices do for you? It can determine your outcome for the day, how you respond to situations, your attitude, your opportunities, your responsibility, your discipline, your accomplishment, and your success. This book is the perfect example, ninja. Every one tip in here that will help you study, strike and succeed is as simple to do as it is for you to make the choice and say, "I will do this." I will turn off the television. Turn it off. I will not hit the snooze button. Don't hit it. I will study for 30 minutes tonight. Study. I will determine my outcomes. Do it. If it's meant to be, it's up to you.

Ninja One Touch Knock Out Power Move
Start small. Today, take 100% ownership and responsibility for your life one step at a time. Pick something in your world you want different, write down what you can do to make it different, and everyday do not go to sleep without making sure those to dos are checked off. Make the choice.

Ninja in Training Challenge
Any new choice requires the ability and the audacity to break out of our comfort zones and be okay with letting go of a past way of doing things. Embrace change, embrace the feeling that comes with bettering yourself. It takes effort and sometimes it will suck, but young warrior, challenge turns to opportunity. Choice turns to change. Change transforms to being a bigger, better, more equipped you.

⛩ Reflections from a Dojo Master

Hello, young grasshopper. You come seeking
wisdom and guidance, it shall be rewarded.

Some choices are harder to make than others, especially when it comes to peer pressure, friend groups and doing what's intuitive to you. Here's a 7 step guide to making the tough choices in your life.

1) Identify who you are, what you want to represent personally, and set a value to all of those character traits. What do they mean to you? How do you want to be perceived? And what is the legacy and memory you want to leave behind?

2) Lay out all of the possible results on both tracks.

3) Picture the situation: What is the ideal desired outcome and personal emotion you want to have when leaving the situation?

4) Approach the situation as if watching a movie. Sometimes you need to take yourself out of the picture. I call this the chick-flick effect. I love watching 'chick'-flicks. I think they are intense! The thing about a chick-flick is there is always a moment in the movie where you know one of the main characters is making a STUPID choice that makes you want to grab the person, shake them and tell them to get their head on straight and not screw up the opportunity for TRUE LOVE (I get fired up thinking about it)!!!! Sometimes you're life is like that- if you were watching the movie of you, what would you tell the character to do!

    a. If you are having trouble doing this, find a sounding board of people to share their thoughts. The secret to getting other people on boards is that

YOU MUST AVOID THE DRAMA-MAMAS! They get more caught up in the emotion than you and will give you bad advice.

5) Slow Down. Be Rational. Get Real. If you react emotionally, you'll be off the hook and not in a good way—in a do-more-damage-to yourself-than-you-want-to kind of way. Take time to reflect and breathe.

6) Be confident, optimistic, enthusiastic not weak, afraid and timid. If you're going to make it happen, make it happen in a confident way. You know, "Move confidently in the direction…"

7) Ultimately, when you finally know what's right, you need to take action. This is often the hardest thing to do. It's hard to let go of a major that offers security, it's hard to say good by to neg-head downer friends, it's hard to do what's right in a times of challenge, it's hard to be uncomfortable. But ultimately action is what moves mountains.

Bonus Follow Up Steps:

8) Think about what the outcomes will mean for you moving forward. What does it mean for your personal meaning, future, and/or as a story you'd share with your kids. Did you make the right choice?

9) Journal about it. The more you reflect on what you did in this time of challenge, the easier it will be to do the right thing in the future.

To your success, grasshopper.

Ninja's Control Doubt

"If we are ever in doubt about what to do, it is a good rule to ask ourselves what we shall wish on the morrow that we had done."
Ninja John Lubbock

Ninja Philosophy

- **Ninjas take action despite doubt**
- **Ninjas bring doubt...doubt that you saw them because you can't see them, they are un-see-able**
- **A ninja is not shackled by fear from possibility; they eat chains for breakfast and kick butt in possibility**

Doubt is like a crappy little moth that bobs and flaps and bobs and flaps at a bright light in the night. Catch that moth ninja. Catch it in the palm of your hand and the squeeze the life out of it. Remember, we're not promoting cruelty against nature; moth is a metaphor for doubt. CRUSH DOUBT, WARRIOR DRAGON! NINJA, CRUSH IT. You are the ninja fly swatter. Doubt is the moth. Do what you need to do, otherwise it will continue to pest.

There will always be fear and discomfort; it will never be deleted from your life. For that, continue to act on your courage and the goal at hand.

Ninja Shadow Master Secret
Master your mind and you control your destiny. You aren't going to get that A because of positive thinking; but you sure as hell will feel a lot better going into that test with the right attitude. Feed a positive sense of personal psychology and empowerment.

Enemy of the Ninja

Trust yourself. It's uncanny how many people know the right thing to do or say at any given time, but choose not to because they don't want to stand up and speak out. Don't run with the heard; there will be times you must go against it because in your true sense of integrity and self; you know the right thing to do. Do it for none other than yourself to be true to you.

Ninja Explains CONTROLLING DOUBT

Trust yourself. There are going to be a lot of moments in your life where either you won't have the time to gather all the information or all of the information isn't going to point to the 'right choice'. In either of these moments you're going to have to trust yourself and make a choice. If you don't choose, someone or something else will regardless of your intuitive feeling. You must 'trust your gut'; and then confidently take action towards it. Sometimes there will be resistance and sometimes your choice will be unpopular; but you must always trust yourself and act on your greatness for what's best for you. When you sell yourself short, the only one that loses sleep at the end of the day is you.

> **Ninja One Touch Knock Out Power Move**
> Develop the power of ready, fire aim; not ready, aim, fire. There are times in your life where planning and careful thought is critical success; there are also times where you spend too much time thinking or aiming, doubt sets in and then you never fire. Start to identify when to plan and when you just need to act.

Ninja in Training Challenge

When in doubt, take flight. You must act. Just act. Ninja, nothing will ever be perfect, you won't always have the answers, you will face evil polar bear-lion-dragons that you've never faced before, you will doubt, question, regret, and more. You're entering new journeys, you're exploring new grounds, you're using new skills, competing with new ninjas. There's a lot of new and a lot of room for doubt. The only way to defeat doubt is to act. Do something. Do something. Do something. You have everything you need to succeed, it's up to you to use it.

Ninja's Optimism and Attitude

"There is nothing either good nor bad but thinking makes it so."
Ninja Shakespeare

Ninja Philosophy

- o **Ninja battling can be a pain in the butt; you can still enjoy the battle**
- o **Ninja may look dark on the outside; but ninja is calm, collected, upbeat and enthusiastic on the inside**
- o **100% of why it's cool to be a ninja starts with one thing, a ninja knows they are a ninja and don't give a rusty dart of what you think**

That's right, world. Ninja, do your thing. Live your life and to hell for all those naysayers! If you don't walk the walk and talk the talk of the ninja; then you'll never be the be that you want to be. No ninja ever went into any battle with the attitude of 'what if I lose this one'. Ninjas go into everything with the 'I got this' attitude. 'I got this' as in 'I got this snake by the head', 'I got this bull by the horns', You got this, so act like it already.

How you show up, is what we pay attention to.

Ninja Shadow Master Secret

Optimism isn't the answer to your problems, but it sure does help. The challenges life will present you are amazing, and it's better to go through hell with a smile on your face than it is to get there and dwell on how bad it is.

Enemy of the Ninja

"I'll be happy when…" "Things will be better if…" I'm not ready until…" stop putting potential on hold. The journey is 99% of your life, enjoy it and wait for the rewards. Enjoying the journey is possibly the single most beneficial thing we can do for ourselves. Focus on the goals and understand that life is a journey, it's a process, it's always happening. If you are saying, "I won't be happy until x, y or z," then you have a long road ahead of you! Life is here to enjoy, to take in, to observe, to appreciate. You will have up days, you will have down days, but the more you take conscious effort to look at life as a roller coaster, a daring adventure, an opportunity to truly LIVE, ADD VALUE, and CELEBRATE, the easier and more fulfilled you will be. Don't postpone your joy and fulfillment, make the choice to be happy and fulfilled now.

 ## Ninja Explains OPTIMISM AND ATTITUDE

Success starts with attitude. How do you hold yourself? What kind of charisma do you bring to a room. Are you constantly going through life like a mega black hole that drains a room of its life and energy or are you the person that people notice because you enter a situation with flare and presence? Develop your attitude to take on challenge. Bring the ability to put negative things into perspective for yourself and those around you. Become a person you would want to be around.

Optimism helps significantly. Optimism is not the ability to say, "Everything is okay," or "This too shall pass." No! Optimism is the ability to see the mountain of an obstacle and say with enthusiasm and conviction, "We can overcome! We will get through this. It's going to suck, it's going to mean late nights and early mornings, but damnit, if we made it this far, we're going all the way."

Ninja One Touch **Knock Out** Power Move
Be grateful. So grateful. Appreciate the abilities and the opportunities and the things you have in your life. You woke up, you can think, you can talk, you can breathe, you can appreciate the design of a flower. Start appreciating the good.

```
Ninja in Training Challenge
```
For the next 3 days, challenge yourself not to complain. Did you know that negative thinking is an instinctual habit in most human beings. You don't believe me? If a baby doesn't like the taste of the food you are feeding it, does it keep eating, or does it scrunch up its face in disgust? As a child, if you didn't like what was on TV, did you make the most of it, or did you complain about it? No one had to teach you to complain. "I don't like" seems to be a phrase that was just as much with us as our fingertips were when we were born. What does this mean? It takes a conscious effort to overcome our instinctive negative feelings; negative feelings which lead to complaining, which leads to more stress and burdened relationships.

Ninja's Strike When the Iron is Hot

"If you really put a small value upon yourself, rest assured that the world will not raise your price. If we all did the things we are capable of doing, we would literally astound ourselves."

Ninja Thomas Alva Edison

Ninja Philosophy

- A ninja that does not act is no better than a mime
- To fly, an eagle must take flight. For a ninja to fly, he must…you know…start flapping! Just standing around isn't doing anything for you!
- If you're in the moment, TAKE THE MOMENT

Do you know what vultures do? Vultures get hungry, and they wait. Then they get more hungry, and they wait. Then they see some other animal make a killing, and vultures come to peck at the remains of the dead, gone, old, rotting carcass. Descriptive enough for you? Sounds like a glorious lifestyle.

Eagles, however, are different, they get hungry, they soar, they dive, they catch, they eat, and they don't wait around for anyone's leftovers. Ninja, when the hunger and desire to do something scratches at you, when that intuitive impulse calls at you for more, LISTEN TO IT! ACT ON IT!

Don't wait. Don't hesitate, or you'll be left picking at the scraps.

Ninja Shadow Master Secret
Time is yours, what you do with it is up to you. One step towards a goal is more valuable than a million years of thinking about it.

Enemy of the Ninja

The adrenaline rush of procrastination. You know what that's like, ninja. You love adrenaline. The deadline is looming. Twelve page paper due the next morning by 8:00am. You haven't even started and it's 8:00pm. You're confident in your skills, so confident, in fact, that it's okay if you check your emails, return some phone calls, and catch up with the roommate. Now it's 9:30pm. Still haven't started. No worries, this is what makes life worth living, you're a ninja, you were made for these moments.

As much as you think you can handle this and it's kind of fun to say, "Still haven't started my paper, but I have this under control." This habit you are forming will come to significantly hurt you in the long run. If you chase two rabbits, you'll end up catching none. Eventually, you'll have three tests, two papers and a group project all in the same week due to procrastination. This week will not be fun for you. Don't procrastinate, it will never allow you to produce your best work.

Ninja Explains STRIKE HOT, NOT COLD

Ninja, you must master your intuitive voice and allow the moment to drive your action. If you have a great idea, act on it! The more you do this, the more confidence you will build, the less stress you will have, the more you'll accomplish, and the more effective you will be. Great benefit comes from great and massive action. You must act! No ninja I know ever just made a kill because they thought about it. Use what you have, act on your thoughts, and eliminate "I should do this…" Just DO IT! Strike when you feel it. The time or circumstances might not be perfect; doesn't matter, STRIKE! Don't let the feeling go cold! Don't let the adrenaline fade. STRIKE! DO IT!

Ninja One Touch Knock Out Power Move
Develop lists. Nobody messes with a ninja with a list. Every idea, every thought, every "I should" you put on a list and at the when the feeling is right, start crossing those things off. This will help prioritize and organize and GET STUFF DONE!

Ninja in Training Challenge

Watch out for weak moments. When atop the mountains of positive momentum, success and a few victories, it's easy to stay the course. The days where unexpected obstacles rear their heads, or the times when you say, "What's the worst that could happen if I don't do this for just one day?" Are the moments you find yourself allowing discipline to slip. Let it slip once, and you'll let it slip again.

Quick Tip

Most people lost their audacity because they have so many run-ins with the 'law of diminishing intent'. The law of diminishing intent says that the longer you wait to do something from the initial time of inspiration, the harder it will be to start that something or gain any momentum towards it.

I have this major project to start and I have this fantastic idea! I can't wait to get started. Then the day gets away from you. "I'll start it tomorrow," you say. Second day happens, you lose some of that initial flare and you say, "That's okay, I didn't plan on starting today anyway. I can start this weekend." The weekend comes, and it's like, "School? No way!" Two weeks go by, you lose the excitement, you lose the idea, the intention and the drive to make it outstanding.

Don't let the law of diminishing intent settle in.

NINJA'S NEVER STUCK

*"So often time it happens, we all live our life in chains,
and we never even know we have the key."*
Ninja The Eagles

NINJA PHILOSOPHY

- o **Ninjas can fly; a ninja is never chained to location**
- o **Ninjas are free; a ninja is never controlled by others**
- o **Ninjas can escape anything, all they have to do is blink**
- o **Ninjas are incredibly creative and elusive, elusive like a fox**

The secret to all things ninja is to understand that where the wind may go, the ninja may go also. The ninja is not tied to an event, place or people. The ninja can journey, explore and experience all that life has to offer.

Chances are you will say someday, "There's nothing to do." If you have a personal purpose and mission, there is always something to do.

> ### Ninja Shadow Master Secret
> Practice doesn't just apply to sports and theatre, it applies to everything. If you want to be a champion, act like a champion. Ninja always has something to do because Ninja is always doing what he/she loves in order to get better and truly master his/her art.

Enemy of the Ninja

Lack of creativity is like a disease that curdles the blood and turns any lively interactive ninja into a ninja zombie "Booooored. Booooooooored." They go through the motions as life passes them by. Read more books, exercise more, have deeper friendships (even if ninjas don't need friends), run up the side of a building. Do something! Energy and creativity must be released!

Ninja Explains NEVER STUCK

It's easy to feel like there's nothing to do; the truth is that there is more to do than you can imagine. With as much responsibility and class work that you have in college, these years will really be your time to explore, learn and grow by pushing your abilities, taking some risks, and creating opportunity. Of course, you won't truly understand this until after college when finances get tighter, responsibilities grow, and skipping work is much different from skipping class. Everything you've ever wanted to do from travel, to starting an organization, writing, learning scuba or a different language, learning from mentors, volunteering, just having fun, are all available to the college student. Take advantage!

Ninja One Touch Knock Out Power Move
The feeling of stuck comes from not being in the right physiological, psychological or emotional state. Ninjas are always in state. They are state. Self-motivate! Learn what it takes to engage you in an activity or towards a goal.

Ninja in Training Challenge
Destroy 'should'; cultivate 'will'. "I should study;" won't set you up to get the job done. "I should really do something;" and they never do. Should doesn't make anything happen. The ninja that sets out on "I Will" usually gets more out of life and college.

QUICK TIP

When you choose the path...

When you decide to enter a path that is focused on your goals and on bettering yourself to be the master ninja that you can be, doors of opportunity will swing open. It's funny, but it's true; when you begin to challenge your comfort zone, and go beyond yourself to grow and gain, you begin to stand up and stand out more than the average bear and people take notice. Professors will be more inclined to talk to you, other students will be more open to learning from you and helping you, and your network will strengthen exponentially.

The thing is that going outside of the box to better yourself is not an average practice, it's unaverage, it's rare; and when you demonstrate an ability to be different in simply your own self-improvement, people will want to learn and be a part of what you have happening.

When you stand out, people notice, they want to help, and they want you on their side.

New potential, new opportunity, new world of possibility.

Go forward ninja!

Study, Strike, Succeed

Ninja, get this done with the focus of a mongoose.

What is the difference, if any, between loneliness and being alone?

_____

_____

_____

How do I manage being alone?

_____

_____

_____

I'm the only one here this weekend, what do I do? How do I feel? What do I think?

_____

_____

_____

Are their activities I've wanted to participate in or groups I've wanted to join that I haven't because I don't have any immediate friends to go with?

_____

_____

What is holding me back from stepping outside of my comfort zone?

_____

_____

What do I need to do to get out of my comfort zone?

_____

Do the potential rewards outweigh the feelings of being uncomfortable?

_____

_____

What will it take for me to be absolutely happy right now?

_____

_____

_____

What do I complain most about?

_____

_____

_____

At what point will I believe to have complained enough, get over it and move on with my life?

_____

_____

_____

So far the complaining has solved:

_____

_____

Personal Notes from This Section

_____

_____

_____

Questions I still Have

_____

_____

_____

_____

How I intend to get answers

_____

_____

Things I want to discuss with a professor, mentor, or advisor.

_____

_____

To improve in my ninja skills and to better my abilities of becoming an ultimate success ninja, I will take it upon myself to follow through on the following discipline/commitment/action each day this week:

_____

_____

I understand that it may not be easy, it may be a little different, but if I'm to truly master the art of nin, then let the above statement be burned in steal by the dragon of a thousand daggers. I will complete by the end of the week.

Fifth Skill Set

Academics

If you didn't know academics were a fundamental skill set to college then I'm glad I am the one who has the opportunity to introduce you to them.

Now, I will first preface with my professional opinion. Notice the word opinion. Wait, before I get to my *opinion,* let me first start off with a question. Since getting into college, have you thought about the relevancy of your high school GPA? I haven't either. Now, take a step back and let's think about your college GPA? Do you think it will have much relevancy three years out of college?

Before I receive some major red flags from parents, academics and achievers, let me plainly state that I think your grades are of huge importance to your credibility, honors and accolades, scholarships and demonstration of knowledge; however, I've met with hundreds of employers, none of which understand how GPA translates to skills learned. The only thing most hiring professionals understand is that high GPA = committed student; it doesn't extend much further from there (unless you are looking to get into grad school after college which is a whole other can of worms). For this next section, be prepared for one major theme, one major take-away, one major mindset that will help you 10 fold through college: ***Grades are not enough.***

It is your responsibility to do more than just study and test. It's your responsibility to build your resume. It's your responsibility to develop competencies beyond just the grades, and this section will take you there.

Ninja's Study Now and Later and Always

"The bitterness of studying is preferable to the bitterness of ignorance."
Anonymous Ninja

Ninja Philosophy

- Ninjas that don't study try to get other ninjas not to study either
- Ninjas with no psychic ability should not depend on their psychic ability to pass tests

Ninjas don't study the typical disciplines like literature, mathematics, physics, or business; they study flying, running up walls, spinning slowly mid-air, shadow art, bicycle kicks and nun chucks. Although the skills of a ninja are essential to our changing times; it is important for the ninja to stay modern and up to date with the culture. A ninja is an expert in anything it does. Whether it be math, the sciences, theatre, business, or psychology, when a ninja strikes, it strikes hard.

Studying isn't just to pass the test. Studying takes you down a path of credentials, expertise, knowledge and understanding.

> ### Ninja Shadow Master Secret
> There is always something to study. The world moves fast, technology and new developments and trends evolve faster than a ninja strike. Well, almost as fast. To maintain your striking ability, you must consistently challenge yourself to sharpen your skills and study outside of what is required of you.

Enemy of the Ninja

Cramming the night before. It may look innocent; but it's capable of mayhem and anarchy. Ninjas know how to maximize their brain capacity to the point where they can physically change into tigers. Can you do that? No? Well, until you can, cramming the night before won't get you the As.

Ninja Explains STUDY ALWAYS

It's always easier to maintain good grades, ALWAYS, than it is to go from low grades to better. It's easier to stay above ground than to dig yourself out! If you miss with the sword, you won't have time to learn how to use the dagger. You have to know them both, less parish at the hand of another. You need to learn how to learn fast. Absorb knowledge. Sometimes you won't have the opportunity to pause and learn a new skill. College is the time to learn how to learn, not after. In your future jobs and careers, you'll be required to learn new skills, take on projects that you don't have experience in, and add value to the opportunities presented to you! In all of those circumstances, you must have the ability to learn, research, know how to find knowledge and strategies.

Ninja One Touch **Knock Out** Power Move
Take Notes! Take notes really well with headings and subheadings. Your memory is not trustworthy. Like the cherry blossom that returns in spring; your mind can come back after reviewing the spring of your notes. Write everything down and study beyond what you think you'll be tested on.

Ninja in Training Challenge
Make your daily study routine daily the same time, same place, same conditions, same environment, EVERYTHING! It's best to find a quiet, peaceful environment where you'll be focused and not distracted! Also! REST! Rest has been proven to help retention by up to 50%, so you take a ten minute walk or rest after learning a new skill or set of information. Treat this personal study period like you would a student organization or class! You don't schedule things over it, and you show up every time!

Reflections from a Dojo Master

Hello, young grasshopper. You come seeking
wisdom and guidance, it shall be rewarded.

How to Take Notes:

This is a personal art form of sorts, depending greatly on how you learn
best. However, many students come into college without the first clue of how to
take notes and how to keep up with a fast paced lecture. Professors do not want
to pause their lecture so that you can write perfectly neat full sentences about
their material. Learn to write quickly enough in legible writing, and if you prefer
your notes to be clean and neat, re-write them later (which will increase your
understanding of them anyway). Learn abbreviations like pg for page, attn for
attention, impt for important. Don't write out every word- the, a, it, she/he, etc.
shouldn't appear in your notes. This should be shorthand, quick, and just enough
to jog your memory of important ideas. Underline or star things during class and
highlight after. In general, keep it quick so that you can pay more attention to
what is being said in the moment than on what you are writing.

From a lecture:

Follow along with what the professor is saying. It's never a good idea to write
down every word, or you won't remember half of what was actually said. Write
down key words or phrases, and broad concept ideas with just enough detail to jog
your memory after class. Leave space next to anything you write down. Then,
immediately after class, during a short break during the lecture, or as soon as
possible, fill in your notes with whatever that key word or idea brings to
mind. This will help you review things to better hold them in your mind long term,
and it will keep your notes detailed enough so with further study you can recall
exactly what was said during the lecture. Keep in mind, if you are ever confused

on what you wrote down or can't recall enough information, use the book, other classmates, a teaching assistant, and of course your professor as a resource to review any concepts.

From a Power Point Presentation:

Chances are you have some type of handout to follow along with. If not, you at least have a clear visual at the front of the room. Copy down or follow along with the visual. But, this is not enough for your notes. This is similar (or should be) to the key words and concepts you write down in the lecture note taking format. You still need to fill in other information in order to have enough to study from.

From the Book:

This is a whole different world of note taking because you don't have to keep up with anybody talking. Read through the headings of your readings and mentally note some bolded words. Also read any chapter introduction or summary information. Look at pictures and gather a strong understanding of what your reading is about before you even start it. Once reading, take notes of headings so you can easily locate the content you are taking notes on. Write down broad concepts and ideas and take notes on their meanings, *in your own words*. Do not copy the book word for word. Go slowly, and write down questions that come up in your reading. Afterward, make sure you find out the answer from a classmate, teaching assistant, or your professor. Also after your reading, write a short summary (about a paragraph) of the most important concepts you learned about.

From a movie:

Movies can be challenging to take notes on if you don't know what is important or what could be tested. In general, I recommend writing down a quick sentence or two, or noting a few concepts or ideas every 5 minutes or so. This will give you a general play-by-play of what happened, summarize important concepts, and refresh your mind as to what happened throughout the movie.

From a speaker:

Similar to a lecture, write down main concepts and ideas, key words and phrases, and just enough detail to jog your memory. Also, jot down questions to ask at the end if there is some sort of Q & A. Or, ask for a way to best contact the speaker if you would have follow up questions. Often, you can ask a professor ahead of time what important concepts or testable material they would like you to pay most attention to.

 To your success, grasshopper.

Ninja Choosing a Degree

"One's work usually occupies more than half of one's waking life. Choosing work that does not bring happiness will lead to a life that is mostly disappointing."
Ninja Bo Bennett

Ninja Philosophy

- **A ninja without a degree doesn't pick classes, classes pick him/her**
- **Get a degree.**
- **Ninjas don't submit to pressure; but at $20,000 a year, every undeclared year that passes is a tough battle to fight**

Times have changed drastically, and what was once considered the noblest profession, being an assassin, is considered taboo or immoral. The ninja needs to use his skills towards a modern profession, he/she can still assassinate; just not people, but deficits, customer needs, social services, management, research. Assassinate the hell out of that stuff. Each beast, however, is not the same as the previous; each requires different understanding and weaponry which will be demonstrated in your degree choice.

Ninja Shadow Master Secret
Ninja does not allow emotion to disease the mind in making decisions. You may love the idea of being an actor; you may also not have an acting bone in your body. Love the thought of being a doctor, but the thought of chemistry scares you? It's time to move on. Do something you enjoy and that you're good at.

Enemy of the Ninja

Picking a major isn't a joke. It's not a 'whatever' type thing. The longer you go without knowing what you're working towards, the easier it will be to not value your opportunity to education. Admit you have a fear of commitment or that you're indecisive, then get over it and figure it out. Ninjas aren't afraid to visit the cave of the career counselor. This isn't a spiritual vision quest; this is a sit down and make a choice type thing.

Ninja Explains **Choosing a Degree**

There are a lot of people out there that will tell you that your choice of degree doesn't determine your career or outcomes; now that's true, but the right degree sure does open a lot more doors in the career field of your choice than if you have a completely unrelated degree. Yes, there are many examples of successful people with successful careers in a field completely unrelated to their degree; but compare that to the people that have jobs in the field they studied. Choosing a degree is a big choice! It takes exploring your interests, assessing your life goals, and understanding the lifestyle you desire.

Ninja One Touch Knock Out Power Move
Talk to a career counselor. This service isn't utilized enough by students. Outside of college, you're looking at a $400 investment to meet with a career counselor. Do it while you have access to it. Talk to as many people as you can.

Ninja in Training Challenge
Be sure. Once you have an idea of what you want to do in life, find three professionals from different companies that are living your job. Ask to shadow them and see if it's what you think it is. This isn't like high school where you take Spanish for two weeks, decide you don't like it and drop. Nope, if you quit two weeks in, you are fined for dropping a class. If you change your mind two years into it, you're going to be in school for 1-2 years more. Find something you'll love to do.

REFLECTIONS FROM A DOJO MASTER

Hello, young grasshopper. You come seeking
wisdom and guidance, it shall be rewarded.

The biggest challenge for many students entering college is that they truly don't
understand the possibility of turning their passion into a full-fledged business or
career opportunity. Students don't understand the almost unlimited potential to
what they can do, explore and seek training in.

So many students I meet love the outdoors and teaching and don't understand
how that fits Adventure Education or Outdoor Education. I meet people passionate
about design but have been told there is no money in it, so they don't go down
that path. Tackle design and business or Industrial Design, pair it with a Real Estate
Degree, sell houses and consult as a designer. Another student is intensely excited
about movies and the impact they make on our culture, explore the world of Film
Studies. She wants to be in the arts and doesn't have an artistic bone in her body,
check out Arts Management. You like photography, start a business. There are so
many options and too many students neglect to talk to a career counselor!

The reality is that career counselors know available degrees and courses of study
that you probably don't know. And since your student fees are already paying for
their services, TAKE ADVANTAGE OF THEM!

To your success, grasshopper.

Ninja's Are Involved

"You must get involved to have impact.
No one is impressed with the won-loss record of the referee."
Ninja Napoleon Hill

Ninja Philosophy

- A ninja that's got somewhere to go, is going somewhere
- A non-well connected ninja is always looking to the well-connected ninja for help and guidance
- A frog that sits in the pond alone, misses the party

Ninja! Training is a constant balance between life, training and experience. Life is good for fun. Training is good for foundations. Experience is good for developing mega tiger-dragon-fire skills. Don't just study a pony; BE THE PONY! Don't just study high kicks, DO HIGH KICKS. Don't just study disappearing when in danger; find a group of other ninjas that want to learn disappearing too and join the study group. Involvement is rockness. This section cannot be emphasized enough.

Ninja Shadow Master Secret

Be on a Board of Directors for a nonprofit. Freshman year, pick a small nonprofit you're passionate about. Freshman and sophomore year, be the most involved, and contributing volunteer you can be. Junior year, begin the conversation about the potential to play a larger role. See what happens!

Enemy of the Ninja

Over commitment is the jerk ninja. Students that love to get involved get involved in everything fast and end up burning out and stressing out. Ninjas that chase one rabbit get one; chase five and get none. You will be better served to find the two or three things you really want to gain as much as you can in and focus on getting involved in activities and organizations that will give you experience and opportunity in those specific fields of study/interest.

Ninja Explains GET INVOLVED

Getting involved is incredibly underrated. Faculty and staff at your college will always say "Leadership stuff looks good on a resume," or "involvement on campus looks good on a resume." They lie. Leadership activities and involvement doesn't look good on a resume; they are NECESSARY, ESSENTIAL and WILL ACCOUNT for 80% of your resume after college! Your campus has more activities, opportunities, clubs, associations and events that are provided for one reason: to better prepare you for life and give you what you need to gain! Get involved! Get experience! Get yourself to be the most experienced ninja level possible with the most nunchuck hours under your belt possible. Don't depend on just the classroom, get your hands on doing something more!

Ninja One Touch Knock Out Power Move
Visit your career center, student life, your resident assistant, and a faculty member of your department. Sit down for a minimum of 30 minutes with each to discuss what is available to you to advance your knowledge and experience in your specific fields of interest and study.

Ninja in Training Challenge
Know what it is you're looking to gain from whatever experience you're involved in. Employers want you to demonstrate that you were involved; however, employers want to know what you did when you were involved! Ensure for the sake of your own time and development that when investing your efforts in anything, track and record tangible results, actions and accomplishments. "I was in leadership club." "I was in leadership club and was the project manager for a campus wide activity which raised $10,000 for local charities."

Reflections from a Dojo Master

Hello, young grasshopper. You come seeking
wisdom and guidance, it shall be rewarded.

It's not your professors' to prepare you for the real world, for a job, or for a career; they are responsible to you, not for you. It is your responsibility to go beyond the classroom and learn more, find more, experience more, ask questions and engage in the learning and preparing experience!

It's easy to enter college thinking, "If I just go to class and do well with grades, I'll be set for the dream job, easy money, big title business card."

That's simply not true. Your professors are responsible for equipping you with the ideas, insights, personal experiences, and curricular foundations necessary so that you have a framework and reference point in your industry, they are not responsible for your success, the actions you take, or the characteristics you develop.

It might sound harsh, but that's a big reason for this book! To give you ideas of how you can go beyond the classroom to develop a platform for your success.

When you combine curriculum with the exercises in here...WOAH, young warrior. WATCH OUT! You will be a much desired, and highly paid ninja.

To your success, grasshopper.

Ninja's Internships

"A man who carries a cat by the tail learns something he can learn in no other way."
Ninja Mark Twain

Ninja Philosophy

- **A ninja takes every opportunity to learn by fire not just by theory**
- **Experience is like a butterfly. Once out of the cocoon and off the ground, they don't go back.**

The ninja journey is an experience, not a map. As you make your ninja journey, understand that if you can get some sweet, kick butt, training in the real world, not your fantasy kingdom, you will be well rewarded in the long run. It takes many years to catch a fly with a paperclip. Many years that your future jobs don't want to pay for you to learn. Now imagine if you went to them with said fly already caught between a paperclip. That's something you can hang your ninja hat on.

Ninja Shadow Master Secret

Internships come in many shapes and sizes and they don't need to go by the name 'internship' to bring you amazing experience. Volunteering for local nonprofits and associations can bring you the same benefit, network and life experience as an internship.

Enemy of the Ninja

Some companies will offer decoy internships. They are dangerous, they are tricky, and they sting like bear traps. Careful, even ninjas can get caught in bear traps. As of late, there are laws and policies being put in place that are hindering companies from taking advantage of 'free labor' through internships; but that doesn't mean that all companies have stopped. Before entering an internship, ask all the right questions, know what you'll be expected to accomplish, and have a detailed understanding of tangible results you can put on a resume after an internship. Filing papers for 40 hours is nothing compared to helping implement a marketing plan that yielded a 20% increase in sales. Know picture perfect what you will be doing.

 **Ninja Explains INTERNSHIPS**

Internships and real world experience will greatly increase your chances of finding full time employment after college. Employers want someone that can offer a past with demonstrated results, professionalism, and an idea of how a company operates. One problem often cited by employers is that new graduates lack the practical knowledge and a hands-on approach. Internships increase that preparedness as well as your confidence, motivation, critical thinking skills and communication abilities. Studies have also been done that have demonstrated that students with internship experience consistently out-perform students without the real world experience. Point being, get your internship game face on!

Ninja One Touch Knock Out Power Move
Before taking on an internship, find out if you'll have a mentor. A mentor will often benefit you as they'll be willing to provide guidance long after the internship is over. A good mentor will share their expertise and knowledge, wanting you to succeed.

 Ninja in Training Challenge
Even as a freshman, you're mindset should be, "How can I get real life experience?" Note, it's not, "How can I get paid?" Yes, paid internships are awesome, but sometimes you won't get to intern, you'll have to volunteer. Volunteering can get you the same experience as an internship. Find a nonprofit organization that offers opportunities to learn through volunteering, even if that means making fundraising calls. Saying you made over 600 fundraising calls with 40% turnover is a very positive thing!

REFLECTIONS FROM A DOJO MASTER

GUARANTEE yourself an internship every semester.

Hello, young grasshopper. You come seeking
wisdom and guidance, it shall be rewarded.

A lot of students get into the habit of looking for internships that are being offered
by companies. **STOP LOOKING FOR INTERNSHIPS; CREATE THEM!**

It is hard to intern without being paid; and I understand that. **The rewards of an
internship, however, are invaluable in the long run, especially if you use NINJA
APPROVED Internship Formula.**

1) Write down the 4-6 professional skills you want to learn from a company,
2) Work with a professor to put together an 'ideal' curriculum model for an
internship that will allow you experience in your desired skills and in the field you
want,
3) Identify local organizations (nonprofits especially) that don't typically offer
internships and call the director of the department you want to be a part of,
4) Give them your elevator pitch, "Hi my name is Ninja and I'm a student at [Nin U]
studying [ninja] with the goal to be fully prepared to [goal] through [position] once
I graduate. I was on your website and I was unable to find if you had internship
opportunities available, but I feel very passionate about your organization and feel
I could learn a lot from being in it while adding value. I worked with my professor,
[name], and put together an internship proposal and outline that I would like to
send to you for review if you'd be open to taking on an intern next semester. I'm
not looking for a paycheck; I'm looking for experience, mentorship and a chance to
observe over the course of [x] hours a week. Actually, if it will help, I'd be willing
to pay you $50 for your time over the course of the semester. May I send you my
outline or may I take you out for a cup of coffee where we can discuss possibilities
on a more face to face basis?"

5) Have references and a resume prepared!

REMEMBER! INTERNSHIPS COST COMPANIES TIME OR MONEY OR BOTH! If you are going into this, get serious about the opportunity!!! That's of uber importance! Also, be prepared for a couple of nos...there-a comin, there-a comin. Don't let them bother you. Ninjas don't get bothered. Pick up, dust off, move on.

 To your success, grasshopper.

QUICK TIP
An often unmentioned and unknown possibility for most students is an independent study.

Independent studies are exactly what they sound like. Opportunities for you to identify a missing piece to your academic journey and fulfill that interest through research, projects and reading done by you with the guidance of a professor or advisor. Independent studies demonstrate discipline, responsibility, initiative and a solution-oriented mindset to professors and potential employers alike. In addition, they are great opportunities for you to dedicate a full semester towards developing portfolio piece that will truly stand out among other class work you've done in the past.

Most degree programs require a minimum of one independent study, field work or other independent initiative; at the same time, many do not. Whether or not your program requires an independent study, I highly recommend digging deeper into a personal interest of yours while getting credit towards your degree and career goals. Heads-up, there will be some paper work involved most of the time, and many students aren't given permission to create independent studies until they are of at least Junior (third year) standing.

Ninja's Resources

"It is folly for a man to pray to the gods for that which he has the power to obtain himself."

Ninja Epicurus

Ninja Philosophy

- The deadliest ninjas are familiar with all options available
- The deadliest deadliest ninjas use all options available
- The deadliest deadliest deadliest ninjas make themselves as 'an option available'

A ninja in battle uses every possible resource to their advantage in order to win. And the thing about being a ninja is that everything is a possible resource because ninjas turn house plants into HI-YAs, backpacks into BAM YOUR FACE, and easy mac into DATE NIGHT! A ninja uses what is available to him/her to be a better ninja. Use what's provided to you; you're paying for it either way.

Ninja Shadow Master Secret

Knowledge is power. Learn about what's available on your campus; chances are whatever is available is to your benefit. Some campuses offer seed money to start businesses, some offer grants, some offer professional services that would cost hundreds of dollars after college. Use the stuff.

Enemy of the Ninja

There goes Mr. Ninja, making his way to class. Down the hallway, he sees Ms. Ninja who asks, "Will you be at the concert tonight of Ninja Band?" Mr. Ninja says no. Later, Mr. Ninja sees a flyer for a Millionaire speaker coming to share wealth tips and provide free financial planning after the speech. Mr. Ninja shakes his head and thinks, "I have better things to do." Ninja gets to class where his teacher announces the opportunity to attend a small group discussion with 15 highly skilled and established professionals. His teacher asks if anyone would like to attend and only the little ninja in the front row says yes. You're 'too cool' 'too knowledgeable' and 'too busy' of a ninja to participate in that stuff. Five years later, you want to attend the concert of the same band; $60/ticket. You and your ninja wife want to create a financial plan with a bank; $800/yr. Later, you look to join a Master Ninja group to discuss ideas and to network: $250/yr. You look back at college and say, "I really wish I took advantage of some of that stuff."

 Ninja Explains **RESOURCES**

You pay a lot for college; and here's something that you probably don't know. You pay additional fees that are built in your tuition costs so that you have access to professional and beneficial resources, opportunities and events; not using them is the equivalent of burning money. Utilize, participate and take advantage of what you have. You are meant to experience college, not passively observe. Things like career counseling, conferences, guest speakers, trainings, concerts, exercise classes are all a part of getting the most out of your college investment and will benefit you in the long run. Ninja, don't waste this opportunity!

> **Ninja One Touch Knock Out Power Move**
> It's easy to ignore and delete campus-wide emails and text messages. Don't. Instead, take the 30 seconds to read them and find out what's going on, and then learn more if something triggers a "I should check this out" response.

 Ninja in Training Challenge
Most campuses allow you to invite groups, organizations, events or people to campus! Visit your Student Life or Leadership departments and Student Government, discuss your ideas and why your idea will benefit the campus. Chances are you'll find funding and create an awesome opportunity for yourself and others!

Ninja's Success/Results

I know the price of success: dedication, hard work and an
unremitting devotion to the things you want to see happen.
Ninja Frank Lloyd Wight

Ninja Philosophy

- **A ninja that holds on to one win as their defining win will never know success**
- **Success is like ninja: it's constant, it's always, it's a state of being**

A ninja in motion must stay in motion. Ninja must not stop. Ninja wins like the snake that has 3 eggs in his belly. Regardless of occasion, however, a ninja must continue. Success is not a onetime thing. Success is a state of being, doing, continuing, progressing, and always, always, always growing.

> ### Ninja Shadow Master Secret
> Do your personal best with what you have. If you are going for a goal; give it 100% before you give up on it. You don't want to have to look back on something some day and ask yourself, "Could it have been accomplished had I given a little bit more?" Just like a ninja football player, put everything on the field for the game; leave nothing to chance.

Enemy of the Ninja

Ninja, you must have patience. There are no such things as overnight successes. What do you think those overnight successes were working on before they were noticed? They were putting 100% effort into their growth and results so that when they would finally be noticed, they'd be prepared for the journey to success. Gratification will always be delayed; so while success waits, work hard for it. All successful people are hard workers. Mind you, ninja, 'hard work' doesn't mean 'always work'; hard work means giving full effort to the task at hand. There is no free lunch. Set a goal and do absolutely whatever it takes to get there. You can't cash a check you didn't earn.

Ninja Explains Success

Success takes work. It will take sacrifice. It will take effort. Sometimes it will be painful. Sometimes you won't enjoy doing what you have to do. Sometimes it will be uncomfortable. Success takes work. Graduating college takes work. Getting a paycheck takes work. Building a company takes work. Taking up a social cause and working to solve it takes work. That's just the nature of the game. You get out of life what you put in. A lot of people will tell you that success is a state of mind. And ninja, that's true; but a state of mind is much easier to focus on if you don't have to stress about how you're going to feed your family. You know what will feed your family? Getting results. Results are beyond just a state of mind; results take action. Success is a mental state as much as it is emotional and physical. Don't trick yourself into saying that as long as I'm happy, I am successful. The truth is that in the professional world, it takes effort.

Ninja One Touch Knock Out Power Move
Don't justify your accomplishments against worse situations. If you're income is $30,000 a year, and you want it to be $60,000; don't ever say, "Well at least it's not $20,000," or "I'm better off than 80% of the world." That doesn't matter. Your results are reflective of your standards, no one else's.

Ninja in Training Challenge
Do what others will not do and one day you can do what others cannot do. If there was one sure fire secret to success, one fast track, jump start ticket to your success it is simply doing what others won't do. Longer hours, shorter breaks, waking up earlier, investing in themselves, speaking in public, taking risks, making sales calls, interning for free, going to events that no one will go to. This is the underlying secret to one ninja's success over all others.

Study, Strike, Succeed

Ninja, get this done with the suave of a mint chocolate ice-cream shake.

Find the right organizations to be involved in.

List what types of activities you enjoy.

_____

_____

_____

What size group of people do you want to work within?

_____

_____

What is the culture/environment/attitude of a team dynamic that you enjoy?

_____

_____

What are your friends involved in (if nothing, we have another set of concerns)?

_____

_____

What stands out that makes you want to get involved?

_____

_____

What are meetings like?

_____

_____

What will you take out of it – long and short term?

_____

_____

What will you contribute – long and short term?
_____

_____

_____

Does this fit into your grand plan of where you want to go?
_____

_____

True story. I was the most effective at studying and completing tasks when there was noise in the background. It couldn't be a movie and it couldn't be music. Movies were too distracting. Music was too ADD for me to focus. The thing that I found made me the most effective, and the thing that I do even now while writing this book, is having a discovery channel wildlife documentary on in the background. It's just enough music and buzz to keep me company, but not enough to distract me.

What's your ideal study environment?

Define:

Cleanliness
_____

Location
_____

Time of day
_____

Type of sound if any sound in the background
_____

For how long
_____

Materials You Learn Best From (note, if notes aren't working for you, start audio recording the lectures)
_____

_____

What topics to you want to know everything about? What are the additional resources you can learn from outside of class that will benefit your depth of knowledge?
_____

_____

If you could design a degree, what would it look like, entail, cover, allow you to do?

The career counselor's office is located where?

What is their contact information?

What are their office hours?

What resources do they provide?

What Four People can I speak with about getting involved with extracurricular opportunities that align with my goals an interests?

What three non-profit organizations are easy for me to access that align with my passion and goals and that I can start volunteering with now?

What Leadership Development Opportunities does my campus offer? When are they? Where are they? Have I put them on my calendar yet?

Personal Notes from This Section

Questions I still Have

How I intend to get answers

_____

_____

_____

_____

Things I want to discuss with a professor, mentor, or advisor.

_____

_____

_____

To improve in my ninja skills and to better my abilities of becoming an ultimate success ninja, I will take it upon myself to follow through on the following discipline/commitment/action each day this week:

_____

_____

_____

I understand that it may not be easy, it may be a little different, but if I'm to truly master the art of nin, then let the above statement be burned in steal by the dragon of a thousand daggers. I will complete by the end of the week.

SIXTH SKILL SET

TACKLING THE CAREER PATH

Ultimately, what's it all worth? What do all the short term joys and challenges, wins and losses come down to? Your long term abilities and lifestyle.

I personally coach students when requested to do so, and one of my students was having the most difficult time with college. Ultimately, we had to have the following conversation.

"College isn't about grades. It's not about parties. It's not about degrees and honors. College isn't about studying or living in the library. It's not about your parents, your peers or your professors. College is about one thing; it's about five, six, seven years down the road, when you are feeling stuck, when you are lost in a job that over time has sanded you down, dulled your edge, and maybe even burned you out. College is about being in that moment of feeling stuck and knowing that because of the foundation you set for yourself during your years of skill and competency development, relationship and network building, and the proper attitude towards yourself and your success, you have options. College is about options. Knowledge is power. Power (not the egalitarian/dictator power) of ability is what college is all about. Power to know that for years, you experimented, you tested, you expanded on your limitations to get the absolute most out of college so that instead of being a good fit for a job where you meet the needs on a checklist, you are employable. Employable means you have options. It means you're desired in the marketplace. You can adapt, learn, grow and commit to adding value.

Your interview process starts on day one of college, and for the next four years, daily, you are doing the things that develop and demonstrate that employability. Consider the four years as an audition, not as a private journey. Take on the things in this chapter full throttle and see for yourself how you will stand up and stand out among the masses of other students. These things make a world of difference.

Ninja's Self-Investment

An investment in knowledge pays the best interest.

Ninja Benjamin Franklin

Ninja Philosophy

- Spend a dollar once; spend a piece of knowledge over and over and over and over again to bring in more dollars
- It is not the first layer of steel that makes the sword strong; it's the next one, then the next one, each fold makes the ninja sword that much stronger

Ninja, your journey starts with the first step; to finish the journey, it will require many more steps, sometimes skips, jumps or leaps. The point is that it's going to take more than one step. Sometimes those steps will be easy. Sometimes they will be confusing. Sometimes they will need you to run up the side of a waterfall. Sometimes they will show nothing in return and you will feel like you haven't gained anything. No matter what small step it may be, you must continue to focus on one thing; the goal. Everything you do has a return; continue that investment and complete your journey.

Sometimes you will want to quit because the rewards for your efforts do not come right away; don't quit. Ninja, all good things come with time. Many years are needed before a seed becomes a cherry blossom tree.

Ninja Shadow Master Secret

Invest 30 minutes a day into reading something that applies to your chosen career or field of study that isn't required of you for class. 15 minutes every morning, 15 minutes before you go to bed. By the end of one year, you'll have read 183 hours more worth of materials. That's the equivalent of three extra college credits.

Enemy of the Ninja

Scarcity hunts you, stalks you, lurks over you; and just when you think you're ready to invest time, money or energy into a book, leadership program, event, or any other program that will help you grow, it kicks your head until you say, "ENOUGH, ENOUGH, I don't have ENOUGH!." You have plenty, young ninja. Plenty.

Ninja Explains **Self-Investment**

It'll be easy to get into the habit of saying "I can't." 'I can't' as in 'I can't spend the time' or 'I can't afford that'. Ninja, control your mind and you control your destiny. Understand that you're not spending, wasting, burning, or losing time or money but that you are investing it in your development, growth, education and future opportunities. Take every chance you to learn or gain something new, something that will benefit you, make you think in a different way, or help. That's why it's called an investment; because you put in time or money and then you get back what you put in.

Ninja One Touch Knock Out Power Move
Interview successful people. Surprisingly, many successful professionals are very open to talking to young people over a cup of coffee. Make sure you have your questions prepared ahead of time and make sure that you are the one that invests in the other person's time by covering the cost of coffee or lunch.

 Ninja in Training Challenge
Education and growth is a continuous process that leads to opportunities over the course of time, not immediately. So be patient, be committed, and continue to invest in yourself even if that it's difficult or uncomfortable.

Design a college education for yourself outside of your college so that by the end of college, you have your degree and you're equipped for business and success. Listen to motivational or leadership audios in your car, on your mp3 player, on your laptop. Find opportunities to grow outside of the classroom, but know they'll take effort, sacrifice, and investment.

Ninja's Career Development

The ability to learn faster than your competitors may
be the only sustainable competitive advantage.

Ninja Peter Senge

Ninja Philosophy

- o **The tortoise ninja stays the course and always wins over the rabbit ninja that's too busy hopping from one job to the next**
- o **A ninja that becomes an expert in walking up the side of buildings, can walk up the side of any building no matter how high**
- o **If you want to get better with that throwing star, Ninja, you better take some initiative to learn**

It is the responsibility of the ninja to know what it takes to become a ninja. The ability to wrestle and ride a bear, eat nails, fly, disappear and travel 417 feet in a single jump are all on the checklist of becoming a ninja, and it's ninja's responsibility to learn them all. A ninja's goal should be to understand where they are and where they want to be in 10 years and then take every action necessary to get there. You want to have options as you progress? Then train yourself to be better.

Career development for a ninja will keep you focused on long term goals, not fleeting opportunities.

Ninja Shadow Master Secret

Career development is no one's responsibility other than yours. It's going to take your own initiative to find a mentor in your field, subscribe to association or trade magazines, join organizations related to your career and interests, and study beyond class requirements. Ninja, it's worth it in the long run.

Enemy of the Ninja

Ninja, LOOK OUT! Jobs are all around you waiting to pounce like a tiger on a monkey! Yes, watch out for jobs. You want one! You should want one! They are great for income, and they are great for now, but are you developing skills, growing and setting yourself up for the future? There's a huge difference between a job and a career. A career is the pursuit of a lifelong ambition or the general course of progression towards lifelong goals. A job is an activity through which an individual can earn money. Both can bring wealth, but you choose one.

 Ninja Explains **CAREER DEVELOPMENT**

Career development is as critical as the ability to read, write and communicate but often it goes unaddressed in college. Ninja, learn about career development. You have an entire life ahead of you, what career steps are necessary for you to get to where you want to be professionally. There's a difference between needing to find a job and developing a career. Jobs are come and go; careers are committed investments to your goals through skill and competency development. Find out what you must do and what you must know to get to where you want to go.

Ninja One Touch Knock Out Power Move
Soft-skills are necessary and in demand now more than ever. It is estimated that only 12% of college grads perform soft skills at levels above average. Communication, teamwork, empathy, problem solving, critical thinking are imperative to your career success! Get going on growing!

Ninja in Training Challenge
Remember that careers are built from the things you do day to day to day to day over long periods of time. You don't know when an opportunity to stand out from the crowd will appear. Read and study and listen so that you're ready when a big opportunity comes your way. Create learning programs for yourself. Do what you can to study now, so that you can strike effectively and be the ninja everyone else wants to be.

REFLECTIONS FROM A DOJO MASTER

Design your Future Interview

Hello, young grasshopper. You come seeking
wisdom and guidance, it shall be rewarded.

Design an interview for your ideal position. If you were hiring, what would you ask a candidate? Go beyond basic questions like how much experience do you have, and into critical thinking areas. For instance, if you were interviewing a counselor at a group home, you might ask the following questions:

"What kind of influence do you think you will have on your clients' lives?"
"In what way would your clients ideally describe your therapeutic technique?"
"If you had to pick, what would be the most valuable piece of information you have learned to prepare you for this job?"

After coming up with at least 10 questions, practice answering them, out loud, from your current experience, as well as with experience you hope to have at the end of your college career.

To your success, grasshopper.

QUICK TIP

Subscribe to journals, trade magazines and professional blogs that are related to your field of study and desired career path.

The insider and real world information you can gain in real world time that is not being talked about or delivered in class will serve you well! Don't wait until graduation to be the professional, act like you're the professional now!

How many of your peers do you know are subscribed to publications such as the ones listed above? Chances are that you don't know many. Remember, success isn't difficult, it's different. Don't do the average thing, be unaverage!

The Benefits to Studying Information from Trade Magazines, Field Journals, Professional Blogs:
- Stay abreast of current happenings, news and trends
- Stay up to day on industry leaders and the practices being used to keep them ahead
- Learn consumer habits
- Understand other industries and how they are impacting your industry
- Become familiar with the who is who of your industry
- Learn the needs that you can start preparing for for when you graduate
- Study the groups that are advertising to your industry and why
- Special Reports
- Job Search

A Ninja's Professional Network

More business decisions occur over lunch and dinner than at any other time,
yet no MBA courses are given on the subject.

Ninja Peter Drucker

Ninja Philosophy

- **Although nun chucking is cool; it's not always necessary to get what you want.**
- **If a ninja clan were to fight a ninja, I'd pick ninja clan every time.**

If anyone knows you're a ninja; you better hope to high heaven you don't die. A real ninja doesn't walk around advertising that they are a ninja; instead they show off their prowess through internships, volunteering, attending conferences and participating in class. Don't be a stupid ninja. If you know people in the ninja business, it's best for them to know what you can do.

A professional network is the easiest thing to build in college; it's when you're the most approachable and people don't think you are just selling a product; but you are, you're selling them on you! In addition, 80% of jobs are gained through networking.

Ninja Shadow Master Secret

If a ninja is going to be hanging out with other ninjas, a smart idea would be for a ninja to know ninja etiquette. A lot of students graduate college without the slightest idea of how to hold themselves in professional situations. Find out if your school offers professional etiquette training, if not, talk to career services or

Enemy of the Ninja

If you lack follow up, people won't follow up with you. Meeting people and getting their business cards, names, email addresses is easy. An expert ninja knows they don't even have to go to events to do that; they can hop on the internet and schedule lunch or coffee with hundreds of professionals at all levels of experience. The challenge for most young ninjas is what to do after. What was your goal in interacting with individuals from your professional network? Was the goal accomplished? Are their next steps? Or are you just wasting this person's time? If you set up anything with professionals, be a good steward of their time. Appreciate it, utilize it, and accomplish something. And ALWAYS send a hand-written thank you immediately following the interaction. ALWAYS!

 ## Ninja Explains PROFESSIONAL NETWORK

A clan is better than a nomad. It takes a village to raise a child. Two heads are better than one. One ninja can defeat 100 non ninjas; one ninja is defeated by 100 other ninjas. This is just how the world works. Take on the world, and don't take it on alone. It's important to identify the people that can be an effective member of your team, introduce you to the right people, or point you in the right direction. The larger your professional network becomes, the more options you will possess and the higher your value becomes. Take the time to truly get involved with your professional community; you never know what it will lead to, and it's always better to have options than to not.

Ninja One Touch Knock Out Power Move
Get in the habit of using Microsoft Excel or Access or anything else that will allow you to systematically organize EVERY contact you meet in college. Your maintaining of a personal database will be awesome to keep your contacts organized and top of mind.

Ninja in Training Challenge

Develop your personal elevator pitch. **YOU HAVE 7 SECONDS TO MAKE A FIRST IMPRESSION.** You MUST have a strong, confident and memorable way on introducing yourself. Confidence and enthusiasm are important here. "Good Afternoon, my name is NINJA, I am an arts management major at NINJA COLLEGE because I believe art is important for the soul, I believe business is important for the mind, and I believe there's a lot that can be done for the young people of this world with both." **Lastly, always remember this! A first impression is less about you, and more about making the person you meet feel good.** But remember, a ninja never says they're a ninja.

REFLECTIONS FROM A DOJO MASTER

Hello, young grasshopper. You come seeking wisdom and guidance, it shall be rewarded.
Career development doesn't start when you graduate. It doesn't start half way through your senior year. It starts now and it's a continual process.

Everything from the clothes you wear, to how you speak, to the way you hold yourself, how you keep your work place, the value you add in class, you web presence and your voicemail message are all points of contact that represent you! And with over 10% of companies firing someone over 2010 due to something on their facebook, you better believe they'll hire or not hire you based on something you have up too! Here's a great exercise I tell all my students. Take a look at your VM message.

How does your voicemail message represent you? Is it soft, quiet, laid back and apologetic: "Hey, this is Ryan. I'm sorry I missed your call. I'll get back to you if you leave a message." Or is it strong, confident, and memorable, "Hi! this is Ryan, I am out movin' and a shakin' at UW Green Bay. Making the world a better place. Leave a message and I'll get back to you right away." It is playful and meant to get attention of friends, "Yo, leave your voice. Whatever." There's a big difference between them all. **Remember, your voicemail is an impression of you! How you show up there is ultimately how you would represent yourself in an interview. Best foot forward!**

If you asked me, professionally, what would a real success ninja do on their voicemail, then I'd tell you this: Change your voice mail message every morning! Every morning? EVERY MORNING! Every morning, you hop online, you find a great uplifting quote, and you do this, "[blank] said [quote]. That's something to think about. Today is [date] and unfortunately, I missed your call. If you leave a message, I am confident I will get back to you right away. Enjoy the day!"

Do that EVERY DAY. Not only does it make a memorable impression, it develops a discipline and a habit for you that comes with invaluable benefit. Get creative and add value, even in your vm message.

To your success, grasshopper.

Ninja's are Great Public Speakers

"Be still when you have nothing to say; when genuine passion moves you,
say what you've got to say, and say it hot.
Ninja D. H. Lawrence

Ninja Philosophy
- o **Ninjas influence through their voice**
- o **The wind does not carry your thought if your words are never said**

The number one fear in the United States is the fear of public speaking. Most people don't enjoy it, and only a very small percentage of those that do enjoy it are actually good at it. For a ninja, this is your most powerful weapon. Train yourself in public speaking, connecting with an audience, understanding motivations, and you will be a cut above the rest.

Speak.

Ninja Shadow Master Secret
Toastmasters is a fantastic group that is filled with people that are at your skill level for speaking. It's usually a very low financial investment for membership ($25-$50); and it is a true opportunity to develop your speaking skills, network with professionals, and advance yourself professionally.

Enemy of the Ninja
The ninja that never picks up the sword never develops the skill of the sword. Public speaking is a fear for a lot of people. Rejection, embarrassment, shyness, self-consciousness, judgment are all reasons why people don't like public speaking. Because of all this fear; a lot of people don't even consider the thought of putting themselves out there as speakers.   This hinders people from participating in class and discussions, asking questions, standing up for themselves, sharing their opinions, and beyond. Don't be afraid to put yourself out there; a skill never used will not develop itself. Anyone can be an outstanding public speaker. It takes time and effort.

Ninja Explains Public Speaking

Public speaking is invaluable to your professional success. It is virtually 100% guaranteed that you will have to present yourself through presentation. At every interview you are basically giving a verbal presentation of yourself which will reflect your enthusiasm, confidence and ability to influence others with your words. You'll be asked to give presentations and reports to a team or to clients. You'll be asked to lead meetings or at minimum participate in them. Even if you choose to be an artist and premier your own exhibit; you'll be asked to talk about it at the opening. Public speaking is an asset! A lot of people will say they hate public speaking or are too shy and quiet to present/speak; don't let that stop you.

Ninja One Touch Knock Out Power Move
Greet everyone that you meet. The halls, the classroom, the union, organizations, events, everywhere you go there are people to meet and if you don't share who you are no one will ever know. The more you introduce yourself, the more confidence and comfort you will gain in public speaking.

Ninja in Training Challenge

Don't just take a speech class; take it to the next level and take an acting class. Speech classes are great, but too often they focus on content building versus actual presentation. Content is important, but it's only 50% of the speaking equation. Ninjas continually challenge themselves to expand their comfort zones; you may have never done anything with theatre before, but that doesn't mean that there is nothing for you to gain. An acting class will stretch your comfort zone and truly develop the presenter you are capable of being- one with confidence and that ninja pizzazz.

# REFLECTIONS FROM A DOJO MASTER

Hello, young grasshopper. You come seeking wisdom and guidance, it shall be rewarded.

Speak in a powerful way. STOP QUESTIONING YOURSELF DUE TO HOW YOU TALK! The way in which you speak demonstrates intent, conviction, and confidence. We've gotten to a point in our world where people talk dangerously casually. Too many, 'like's or ending opinion statements with 'I don't know' or consistently saying 'but' in order to not fully commit to a statement. **It comes off as lazy, passive and indecisive.**

Speaking with confidence brings confidence! There are far too many people out there that change their direction every which way the wind blows; you don't have to be one of them! It'll get you in trouble as you easily fall into other people's opinions, peer pressure or directions. Be a leader, not a follower. Start being aware of your language and disciplining yourself to commit to what you are saying.

Eliminate the words but, try, I don't know (when in regards to your personal opinions and thoughts), and um. They will not serve you.

To your success, grasshopper.

Ninja's Develop People

"In learning you will teach; in teaching you will learn."
Ninja Phil Collins

Ninja Philosophy

- Ninjas can replicate themselves 1000 times over
- Share the power; share the responsibility; get things done better, faster, smarter
- When one teaches, two learn

Ninja, this is reals, yo. Be the ninja that can spin kick in the air 19 times before landing; be able to teach other ninjas to do the same and you will be invaluable. People want to learn, grow and be better. Since you're already the best ninja, people will come to you to be better. Ninjas live to serve. That's their call to duty: service to others.

Teaching reinforces what you already know, deepens your understanding of a subject and replicates that in another. The more you give, the more you gain.

Ninja Shadow Master Secret
Learn how to defend your position without getting emotional. Yes! Have Passion! Have Power! Have Enthusiasm when you share your opinions! But don't get angry, bent out of shape or feel like you're being attacked if other people don't like what you have to say.

Enemy of the Ninja

Don't be an island. Yes, you certainly can do a lot on your own, ninja. And sometimes helping others will literally feel as if you are carrying their dropped-dead ninja assassinated butts. There will be days you get frustrated, tired and feel like you have better things to do. But ninja, someday, someone will feel that same dead-weight feeling about you; and the last thing you'll want is for them to drop you. Reach, teach and inspire. You can handle the mission on your own, but much reward comes when you have others to depend on. Delegation is your best friend when others are developed like you!

Ninja Explains DEVELOPING PEOPLE

In college you will be placed in many many group settings which will force you to work well with other peoples. Roommates, classmates, group mates, student organization mates are all environments in which there will be different personality types and skill levels brewing and an objective will still need to be completed. Your ability to identify strengths in others, or guide them towards a beneficial action will be a tool that you must have in your personal ninja weapon belt. The more you develop people and get a handle on it in college, the more effective you will be after college when you're working within a group. If you can be ahead of the learning curve before you graduate, then instead of catching up on learning how to work with and develop people; you'll be able to stay ahead and your boss will notice.

Ninja One Touch Knock Out Power Move
Mentors have been mentioned earlier; but have you thought of becoming a mentor? There are a lot of opportunities for young ninjas out there to join youth-mentorship programs. Be a part of one to build your network, invest in younger generations, build your volunteer hours, and to begin your journey of learning how to teach which is essential to business success.

Ninja in Training Challenge
Everyone remembers that one teacher they had in middle school, high school or college, the one that really stood out from the others because that teacher went the extra mile. Make a list of all of the characteristics that you enjoyed in a teacher like that; make a list of all the characteristics you didn't enjoy in other teachers. Use that list as a template to assess yourself in your ability to motivate, inspire, educate and influence others.

Ninja's See & Take Opportunity

People will judge you by your action, not your intentions.
You may have a heart of gold – but so does a hardboiled egg.

Ninja Anon

Ninja Philosophy

- Ninja can customize training if they don't like the one they are given
- If no one knows you're a ninja open for business; no one will do business with you.
- Non ninjas see challenge, death, despair and end to all; real ninjas make challenge, death, despair and end the beginning of a great story
- No such thing as a lucky ninja

There is always something of value to you, but it won't always be a clear picture. Sometimes you need to create and find the opportunities on your own. Opportunities are EVERYWHERE. And it's not about being in the right place at the right time, it's about being the right person so you can constantly create the conditions for the 'right time' and the 'right place'.

Ninja Shadow Master Secret

Shut doors so new ones open. It's harder said than done. There are a lot of stagnant things in your life that are keeping you at average. They could be habits, they could be people, they could be some classes that just aren't challenging. You must close some doors to make room for new ones to open.

Enemy of the Ninja

Discounting the idea of opportunity is the biggest threat to this topic. If you do not value the real possibility that college and what you create during college is in direct proportion to the amount of opportunities you have after, then you are one blind ninja. And I don't know one blind ninja that can catch an arrow mid-air.

Ninja Explains SEE & TAKE OPPORTUNITY

There will always be opportunities for you. Always. In college, after college, and forever as you move forward opportunity will abound, but it may not always be easy to identify. Opportunity is not about getting lucky; opportunity is about creating a plan for your life that will lend you more favorably towards accomplishing what you want. Every class, every event, every organization, every community association is an opportunity for you to increase your network, get your face in front of people, and share who you are and what you're all about. Take advantage of your opportunity. You never know when someday some person will come to you saying, "I remember your ninja skills from two years ago, and my company has been looking for a ninja like you for some time."

Ninja One Touch Knock Out Power Move
Be a social media ninja! Send some virtual throwing stars through the e-highways and byways of the internet. You want to be up to date with your online presence because you never know what opportunities will come through someone looking you up or seeing your online profile, accomplishments and status.

Ninja in Training Challenge

College isn't just a degree. It's a launching pad for your business. Your business of you. You are building a company, and everything you do is directly tied to the development and growth of that company. So as you go through college, building the foundations of YOU, you have to continuously remind yourself of what this company will look like in the end. What will you have accomplished, what's your network, what's your brand, and what opportunities do you have to show for it? The entire purpose of college is to develop and make available future opportunities to you. Understand that and you won't waste a minute because of lack of opportunity.

QUICK TIP

Market yourself! On a resume, in an interview, on a thank you letter, in an email; always be marketing yourself! This doesn't mean manipulating a message, and it's not about commercial promises..."90% of the time it virtually works all the time."

I tell the students I work with, what kind of salary do you want to earn?

"For starters? Right out of college? Around $34,000 a year."

$34,000 a year? That means EVERY touch you ever make to a company should be a $34,000 touch. Every thank you, every email message, every phone call, every *anything* should be worth $34,000.

Whenever I had to look for a job, I was marketing myself. How do most people apply for jobs? An e-resume or a letter by mail. What do I do? Roll it up, throw it in a coffee mug, send it in a package. Everyone loves a package! How do people send thank yous? With a card or a nice letter. What would I do? Find something out about the interviewer that they enjoy personally: a sports team, a state, a nonprofit, a hobby, something that I can replicate through a trinket, a gift, a replication or a symbol that immediately makes the receiver smile, look at, and put on their desk or at least hesitate before throwing it out.

Always be marketing yourself, it's what will make you stand out.

Ninja's Add Value

"If you have an hour, will you not improve that hour, instead of idling it away?"
Ninja Lord Chesterfield

Ninja Philosophy

- **The loyal and noble ninja excels in not stealing from the world, but in giving to the world**
- **A ninja gives more than they think they can afford**
- **Always at service, always to help, making the world a better place through getting rid of bad guys and using grappling hooks to do awesome things**

To be of service to the world, first and foremost, is the law of the ninja. How may we help? How may we use our ultra-mind powers to bring you peace? How may we take your day from good to outstanding? With that approach, ninja, you and your world will be better.

Ninja Shadow Master Secret
Get a degree in the Study of How to Make Other People's Lives Better. When you network, is it about you or the other person. When you are seeking employment, is it about you or the team? When you are offering your abilities and services, is it about your livelihood or about the improved quality of life for the other person. You may not get credits for this, but find out what it takes to earn this degree.

Enemy of the Ninja
Do not be the firework that sparks, flies and lights up the sky with a 'look at me' attitude. Be more of a firefly that provides more light for a longer period of time. 'Look at me' fades. Eventually people are tired of helping you, they want a more mutual relationship that is invested in them.

Ninja Explains ADD VALUE

There have been a lot of recommendations for you to stand out in. The only way you've made it this far in this book is if you are getting something out of it. It's not about me, it's about you. You'd have never opened this book if it was, LOOK AT ME AND MY NINJA POWERS! We've shared a lot of ideas to truly be different and set yourself apart; but the number one way to truly make yourself stand out is not to enter college from the perspective that you are just some consumer, there to be served, waited on, and with customer service representatives waiting on your beckon call. Instead, enter college with the perspective of how can I significantly impact this campus, the lives of my professors and the lives of my fellow students. Enter college from a place of I'm here to add maximum value to the world after, how do I get started now? How can I contribute more than I consume?

Ninja One Touch Knock Out Power Move
What's your cause? What's worth fighting? What are you doing to get involved with it? We are all skilled and talented with gifts that people and organizations need and will utilize towards a goal. **Something should get you so passionate that every time you think about it, it turns you on to getting something done.** What's your cause? Where do you add value?

Ninja in Training Challenge

Fulfillment comes from adding value to other people's lives. How do you give? Truly give? Meaning outside of your comfort zone and above and beyond what is expected of you. As much as you may not like this, you are a product in the marketplace. If there was no need for you, you wouldn't be here. There is a need for you. Give more to this world than is given to you. Contribute more than is expected of you.

REFLECTIONS FROM A DOJO MASTER

Hello, young grasshopper. You come seeking wisdom and guidance, it shall be rewarded.

What do you do?

I ask this to groups of people all the time. Here is a sample of answers.

I study art. I'm an actor. I'm a TA for the Psychology Department. I am the President of Student Government. I'm interning for a marketing agency downtown. I volunteer with a nonprofit.

Before you keep reading, answer for yourself. What do you do?

Here's another question. Do you care about any of those answers? Do they light you up? Excite you? Do they demonstrate anything out of the ordinary?

When someone gives you the chance to say what you do, come from a place of service.

What do you do?

I allow audiences the opportunity to lose themselves in ninety minutes of emotion, entertainment and powerful human dynamics through acting.

I offer a passionate perspective for psychology to 200 first-year students, while allowing a professor of mine further their research in childhood development.

I put the responsibility of education back into students hands, equipping them with the tools, talents and audacious hunger to break the mold, set their own standard and not regret a minute of their college life ☺ Total ninja speaker.

To your success, grasshopper.

Ninja's Image

Your premium brand had better be delivering something special, or it's not going to get the business.

Ninja Warren Buffett

Ninja Philosophy

- Ninjas look AWESOME!
- What is the brand of a ninja? Ninja. Think it over.
- When a ninja dresses like a ninja; there's no doubt that they are dressed like a ninja

As you continue your journey to become the ultimate study, strike and succeed machine, you must remember, dress to the task at hand. Night mission? Wear black. Day time? Wear normal clothes. Hanging out with other ninjas? Bling out your Hi-Top Tabis. Doing something in a blizzard? Gear up the white. Going to a client interview? Dress the role you want, The fact is you're always the fashionable, stylish, impression-making, trend-setting ninja. Dress-o to impress-o.

How you present yourself should be your best Hi-Top Tabi forward the first time.

Ninja Shadow Master Secret

Have you put considerable thought, creativity and development to your brand? What do you want to convey to an audience and how are you doing that? Is your brand successful in speaking a message? You must take some time to create your brand. Sit in on some marketing or advertising classes or pick up *A New Brand World* by Scott Bedbury.

Enemy of the Ninja

A ninja can be invisible. Invisible means transparent. Ttransparent means that people can see through. See through means they'll know what you know if it's knowable. And if they don't know, if they can't find the information they're looking for, you are replaceable. If a potential client or employer can't learn more about you through more than just your resume, but can learn about your competition. Don't neglect how you represent yourself off of paper.

 Ninja Explains **Image**

The professional world has progressed from corporate brand to product brand to personal brand. As the world becomes more and more competitive; employers and companies are looking for individuals that understand the value of brand, image and web-media. You must be branded, branded, branded. The need for you to truly develop your personal brand is critical to your advancement in any career field regardless of your age or position.   Most of your brand will be conveyed to an employer, company or community via the internet. The internet is more often than not the very first place people look to find information about you. Type in your name into a search engine, what is the impression your online presence demonstrates? Would you hire you based on the info presented? You are the president of your own company, You Co. What's your brand management department doing to make you stand out and give off a great brand impression?

Ninja One Touch Knock Out Power Move
Do you ever notice that when someone is professionally dressed they stand out? They are noticed. People ask, "Where are you going? What do you have going on today?" At any moment you have an opportunity to be in front of potential employers, dress to impress.

Ninja in Training Challenge

In creating your personal brand; there are several things you should manage to ensure similarity, consistency and visibility. Ensure that none of them are neglected as they all work together to demonstrate and educate others on you.

If you don't know where to start on your brand; check out the brand attack plan for ninjas on the following pages. It's time to make a killing out of your brand!

REFLECTIONS FROM A DOJO MASTER

Points of Impression

Hello, young grasshopper. You come seeking wisdom and guidance, it shall be rewarded.

Picture this one, ninja. If someone were to enter your ninja dungeon headquarters (or your room), would it be a pretty site? What if they took a ride with you in your ninja transportation vehicle? What about your web-presence if they typed in your name, what would show up? Every impression is a critical impression, and you never know who will notice and what they'll notice.

Two quick stories. 1) I had a friend that went to a job interview. First thing the potential employer said to him was, "Let's go for a drive." It seemed that this was done in order to have the interview at another location, in reality, the first question was, "How you do anything is how you do everything; how do you keep your car?" Needless to say, my friend didn't get the job. Story 2) A colleague of mine was asked on a date by a guy she just met. She said to me that she always requested that any first date takes her to a specific restaurant where the service is not the best because she said the best way to find out about anyone is to see how they treat a server.

Point...every impression is an important impression. Here's some for you to think about, ninja.

1. A personal business card. Yes, even in college you should have a business card. mydropcard.com or businesscard2.com or vistaprints.com
2. Resume, cover letter, reference page all of which should be well formatted and easily accessible online through employer search engines and through a personal webpage
3. A personal portfolio featuring things you've done or created which you should have as a hard copy and again available online
4. A blog which should address issues and success strategies in the professional world and your career field
5. Facebook, LinkedIn and Twitter or other online accounts should be up to date and respectable
6. Your personal email address shouldn't be your campus email and it shouldn't be HottBod@whatever.com
7. Video resume; do you have any videos posted? What is the message?
8. Wardrobe is important.
9. Work space? Car space? Kitchen? Backpack? Notes? What do they tell me?
10.   Don't email anything you wouldn't share with your mom. Don't text anything you wouldn't want your dad to see. Don't Facebook something you wouldn't want an employer to witness.

To your success, grasshopper.

Study, Strike, Succeed

Ninja, get this done with the dedication of a mama goose.

Research and identify five books that you will read outside of what's required of you in class. The five books should be related to your growth and development. What are they? Don't know where to start, ask a professor, "What would you recommend I read outside of class?"

_____

_____

_____

_____

Identify ten community members to interview that are in the field you want to be in or that could act as a mentor for you. List their names, contact information, assistant's name, knowledge about the company, and any additional notes you may want to keep track of. Take these people out to coffee and take the time to host an informational interview with them.

Name	Company	Email	Phone	Assistant	Other

Earn your additional degree in Personal Development and in How to Make People's Lives Better. What are the titles of five classes you believe would be offered in these degree? What kind of curriculum would you study? What books would you study from to cover the topics?

_____

_____

_____

What are two industry magazines you can subscribe to and 4 blogs you should follow that will help you better understand the ins and outs of the industry?

_____

_____

_____

What are some out of class opportunities offered by the campus or community that will help you develop your speaking skills? Otherwise, is there an acting class you can take?

_____

_____

_____

What are four resume goals that you want to be able to have on your resume by the end of the year?

_____

_____

_____

Employability Assessment

Being employable is different from being able to get a job. Employable means that you offer a variety of characteristics, strengths and skills that are unique, broad and consciously developed for your long-term career growth and achievement. The following exercise will help you understand your employability versus you basic achievement of a degree.

What is the present knowledge that you have that would be beneficial to a career in your field of interest?

_____

_____

_____

What are the current skills you have that are needed in a career and in order to contribute to a team or company?

_____

_____

_____

What are the personal characteristics you have that are desirable for an ideal team member?

_____

_____

_____

What do you need to learn?

_____

_____

_____

What skills do you need to develop?

_____

_____

_____

_____

_____

What characteristics do you need to establish? _____

_____

_____

_____

Strengths Assessment

Ask the following people:

Professor| Advisor | Mentor | Friend | Peer | Family Member

The following questions:

What's my unique ability?

What characteristics make me invaluable to a group?

Where could I improve?

What would it take for me to truly stand out or truly develop my unique abilities or strengths?

Add Value

What Assets do you want to be able to contribute to a team that will make you invaluable? _____

_____

_____

Do you know how to develop those assets? If yes, how? _____

_____

_____

_____

Do you know who you can talk to for guidance on how to develop those assets?

_____

_____

_____

Identify your perfect career and the role/responsibilities that would be ideal for you to have. Include a snap shot of the company culture, the size of the team and the history of the organization.

_____

_____

_____

Research and identify individuals currently working in a role similar to the one above. Set informational interviews with them to ask them if your assumptions about that role are accurate and if they would add any additional information to your assumed profile of the role.
List the responsibilities and assets needed for that role.

_____

_____

_____

Now, try to research and set an appointment with the above individuals' bosses. Give those bosses the list of assets, skills and responsibilities you've identified for the desired position and ask the boss to prioritize them by level of importance. The top three priorities are:

_____

_____

What are you plans for bettering the above three for yourself?

_____

_____

_____

What do you do?

_____

_____

_____

_____

Memorize the above.

Personal Notes from This Section

_____

_____

_____

_____

Questions I still Have

_____

_____

How I intend to get answers

_____

_____

_____

Things I want to discuss with a professor, mentor, or advisor.

_____

_____

_____

To improve in my ninja skills and to better my abilities of becoming an ultimate success ninja, I will take it upon myself to follow through on the following discipline/commitment/action each day this week:

_____

_____

_____

I understand that it may not be easy, it may be a little different, but if I'm to truly master the art of nin, then let the above statement be burned in steal by the dragon of a thousand daggers. I will complete by the end of the week.

Ninja! You Drive!

I have parting words. At least, that's what I believe should go here. And in the spirit of doing things that we should do, I will close with the following.

You're in the Driver's Seat

There is only one person that is responsible for your success, outcomes and experience while in college and after college. You guessed it, it's 100% you. You have support and people and opportunities available to you to assist in those outcomes; but at the end of the day, what you do or don't do is entirely up to you. There is not a line of people outside waiting to take it upon themselves to make the most out of your life for you. Shocking! I know, right? Ninja, this book was designed for you, but at the end of the day....

It's Just a Book

A freaking awesome book if I do say so myself as it's filled with ninja greatness! Ninjas become ninjas through study and practice and action. Notice I did not say, 'ninjas become ninjas by just studying'. They DO stuff with what they studied. YOU MUST INVEST THE EFFORT!

Master Yourself

If you let the world master you, you will constantly be at the will of the waves, the wind and any other little idea that someone else has for you. If you learn to master yourself, you'll be wealthy, healthy, and happy. It's a great way to go. It's hard to master oneself. This is a difficult feat, as you probably know, it's easier to correct others than it is to correct yourself. You must remember, it's hard to give something you don't have. If you don't exercise daily, it's hard to give advice on maintaining your health. If your study skills lack, it's hard to help someone with their tests taking skills. If your confidence is in the sink-hole, it's hard to tell a friend to brush the dirt off their shoulders, get up and move forward. Master yourself. Get yourself together and the world will begin to look, feel and act different.

Thank you

You owe this to you. You owe your possibilities to this world. To not act on the intuitive abilities, the gut intentions, and the gifts and abilities that bring you alive is like stealing from a deserving world and from yearning people that are waiting, watching and looking to you to be who you are and what you can be. Thank you for reading this book. Thank you more for living what's inside of it. Free your inner ninja.

About the Ninja Author

Ryan Penneau is the founder of Take Back College (www.takebackcollege.com) an organization committed to impacting students with tools, strategies and experiences that better equip them to be responsible adults, life-long learners, passion driven contributors to the community and professionally successful (and employable) individuals.

His utmost passion for students is demonstrated through his interactive keynote presentations and workshops that serve thousands of young people every year, equipping them with unconventional success strategies that work in developing a student's capabilities and their curricular knowledge.

Ryan earned his B.A. in Arts Management from the University of Wisconsin- Green Bay and an M.S. in Experiential Education from Minnesota State University – Mankato.

For more information visit www.TakeBackCollege.com or email Speaking@TakeBackCollege.com

Ryan Penneau with Author of Chicken Soup for the Soul, Jack Canfield

A final story

Two fortune tellers to the king sat in their quarters, eating their evening meal.

One of the two was fortunate. He was blessed with abundance and ate very well. As he fed from the bounty his riches could afford him, he said to the other, "Learn to say to the king what he wants to hear and you could be rich like me!"

The other looked up. He too was fortunate and blessed with abundance. He ate well, but did not have the luxury of options and a large bounty of food because he could not afford it. He pulled himself away from his broth soup and responded to the other, "Learn to love broth soup and you would be able to say what you want."

—

Your way of ninja should be a path that you are able to live with, and ultimately a way of life that allows you to live with yourself.

I hope the journey is one of success and fulfillment no matter you make it.